E S T A T E   P U B

T E L F

G000136414

Shawbirch 4 ___ 5 **Admaston**	**Leegomer** 6 **Hortonwood** **Donnington**
Wrockwardine 10 ___ 11 **Wellington**	**Hadley** 12 ___ 13 **Ketley** **Redhill** 14 ___ 15 **Oakengates**
Lawley 16 ___ 17 **Dawley**	3 **TELFORD CENTRE** 19 18 **Stafford Park**
Woodside 20 ___ 21 **Coalbrookdale**	**Stirchley** 22 ___ 23 **Madeley** **Halesfield**
Ironbridge 24 ___ 25 **Broseley**	26 **Coalport**

ROAD MAP   Page 2

TELFORD ENLARGED TOWN CENTRE   Page 3

STREET INDEX   Page 27

Every effort has been made to verify the accuracy of information in this book but the publishers cannot accept responsibility for expense or loss caused by any error or omission. Information that will be of assistance to the user of the maps will be welcomed.

The representation of a road, track or footpath on the maps in this atlas is no evidence of the existence of a right of way.

One-way Street   →
Car Park   🅿
Place of Worship   ✚
Post Office   ●
Public Convenience   Ⓒ
Pedestrianized   ▨
Scale of street plans 4 inches to 1 mile
Unless otherwise stated

Street plans prepared and published by ESTATE PUBLICATIONS, Bridewell House, TENTERDEN, KENT, and based upon the ORDNANCE SURVEY maps with the sanction of the Controller of H. M. Stationery Office.

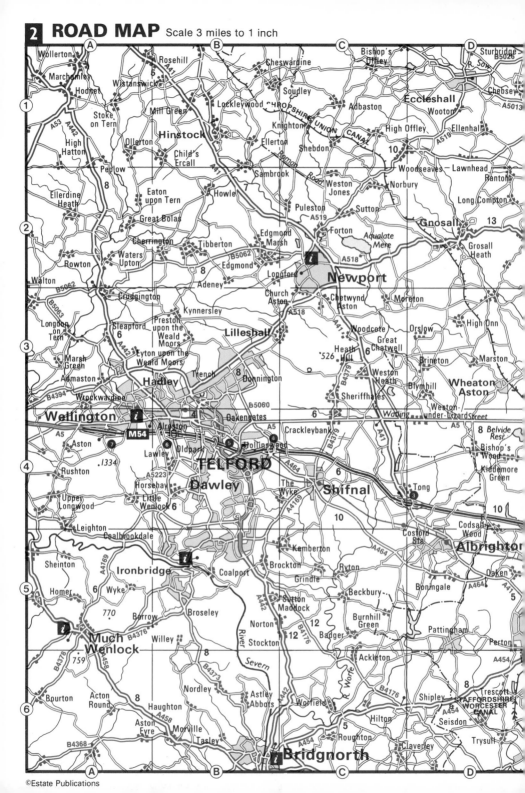

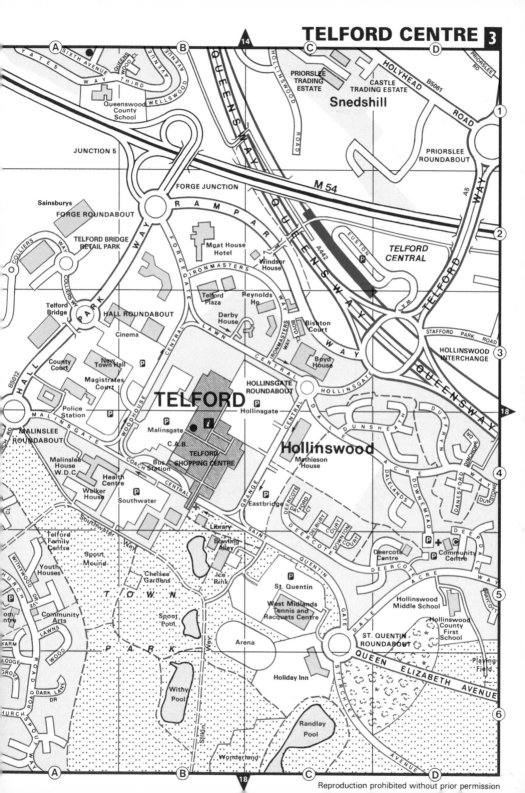

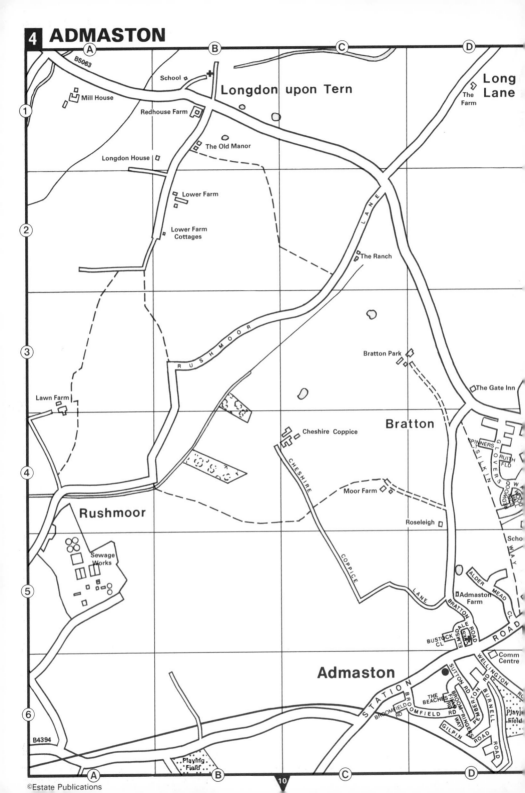

Ⓐ Ⓑ Ⓒ Ⓓ

B5063

Long Lane

School

✝ **Longdon upon Tern**

The Farm

1

Mill House

Redhouse Farm

The Old Manor

Longdon House

Lower Farm

2

Lower Farm Cottages

The Ranch

R U S H M O O R

L A N E

3

Bratton Park

The Gate Inn

Lawn Farm

Cheshire Coppice

Bratton

SPINNERS LA

GLOVERS

RUITH FLD

SILKIN

W

4

C H E S H I R E

Moor Farm

Roseleigh

Scho

WAY

5

Sewage Works

Rushmoor

C O P P I C E

ALDER MEAD CL

Admaston Farm

L A N E

BRATTON ROAD

R O A D

BUSTOCK CL

WELLINGTON

Comm Centre

Admaston

SUTTON RD

WELLINGTON ROAD

BURNELL ROAD

6

S T A T I O N

THE BEACHES

BROOMFIELD

BROOMFIELD RD

RINGERS WAY

GILPIN

EMBERS ROAD

Playing Field

B4394

Playing Field

Ⓐ Ⓑ Ⓒ Ⓓ

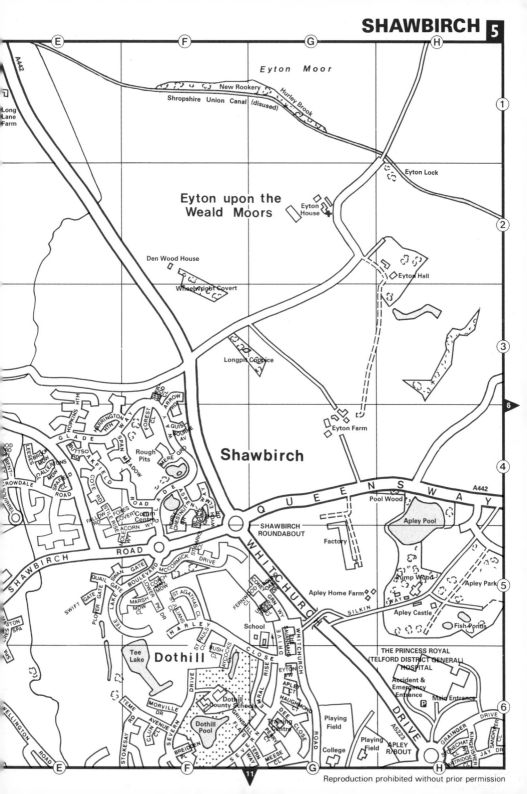

Eyton Moor

New Rookery
Shropshire Union Canal (disused)
Hurley Brook

Eyton Lock

Eyton upon the
Weald Moors

Eyton House

Eyton Hall

Den Wood House

Wheelwright Covert

Longpit Coppice

Eyton Farm

Long Lane Farm

Shawbirch

Rough Pits

Comm. Centre

SHAWBIRCH
ROUNDABOUT

Pool Wood

Apley Pool

Factory

QUEENSWAY

A442

Pump Wood

Apley Home Farm

Apley Park

SILKIN

Apley Castle

Fish Ponds

SHAWBIRCH ROAD

Tee Lake

Dothill

School

St Pauls Cl

WHITCHURCH

Dothill
County Schools

Dothill
Pool

Training
Centre

Playing
Field

College

Playing
Field

THE PRINCESS ROYAL
(TELFORD DISTRICT GENERAL)
HOSPITAL

Accident &
Emergency
Entrance

Main Entrance

APLEY
R/ABOUT

DRIVE

A5223

WELLINGTON ROAD

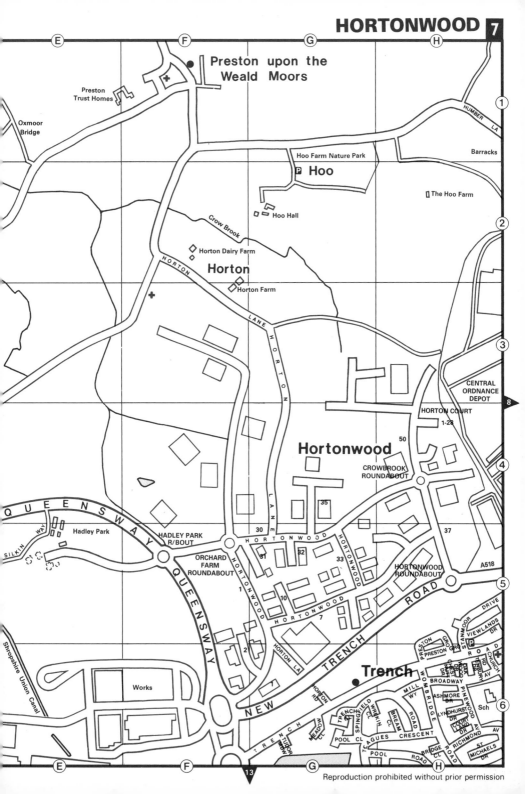

Preston upon the
Weald Moors

Preston
Trust Homes

Oxmoor
Bridge

HUMBER LA

Barracks

Hoo Farm Nature Park

P Hoo

The Hoo Farm

Crow Brook

Hoo Hall

Horton Dairy Farm

HORTON

Horton

Horton Farm

LANE HORTON

CENTRAL
ORDNANCE
DEPOT

HORTON COURT
1-28

50

Hortonwood

CROWBROOK
ROUNDABOUT

35

QUEENSWAY

WAY

SILKIN

Hadley Park

HADLEY PARK
R/BOUT

ORCHARD
FARM
ROUNDABOUT

30

31

32

33

37

A518

HORTONWOOD

HORTONWOOD

HORTONWOOD
ROUNDABOUT

QUEENSWAY

1

10

7

Works

HORTON LA

HORTONWOOD

HORTONWOOD

2

Shropshire Union Canal

ROAD

TRENCH

NEW

Trench

PRESTON
STANMOOR DRIVE

VIEWLANDS
DR

PRESTON GRO

R O A D

CHURCH

TENBURY AV

BROADWAY

MILL
WY

ASHMORE
DR

PINEWOOD

LYNDHURST
DR

WOMBRIDGE

Sch

PRESTON
ROAD

TRENCHFIELD
DR

SPRINGFIELD

WREKIN

BREAM

ROAD

ROAD

BRIDGE
CL

RICHMOND

ST
MICHAELS
DR

MEADOW
CT

POOL CL

TEAGUES CRESCENT

POOL
ROAD

TRENCH
TUDOR WW

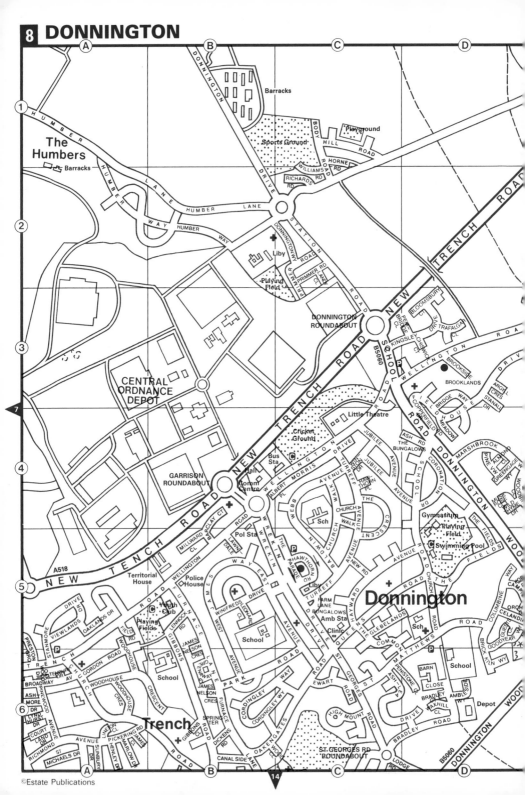

E   F   G   H

Lilleshall

Cricket Ground

Old Farm

1

NEW TRENCH ROAD   A518

Honnington

HILLSIDE

ROCK ACRES

CHURCH MDW

Honnington Bridge

YEW TREE DR

School

Honnington Grange

The Old Hall

2

ROAD

CHURCH

LILLYHURST

Lilleshall Grange

Caravan Park

NELSON WY

SUTHERLAND RD

MERRINGTON

The Oaks

Grange Plantation

3

GOWER DR

DRIVE

Muxton

Playing Field

SALTWELLS DR

SWEET BRIAR

SALTWELLS

SILVERDALE

BROOMHURST

OSTERLEY GRO

GRANVILLE DR

LANESIDE

Sulphur Riefe Plantation

Grange Cottages

ROAD

Abbey Farm

THORNTON

THE PADDOCK

HOLLAND DR

HACKETT WAY

4

RAVENSCROFT

MARSHBROOK

BRANDS

School

Lilleshall Grove

WAY

STABLE

MARSHBROOK WAY

LANE

Muxton Grange

Golf Driving Range

5

WAY

DONNINGTON WOOD ROUNDABOUT

Shropshire Golf Course

New Lodge

6

E   F   G   H

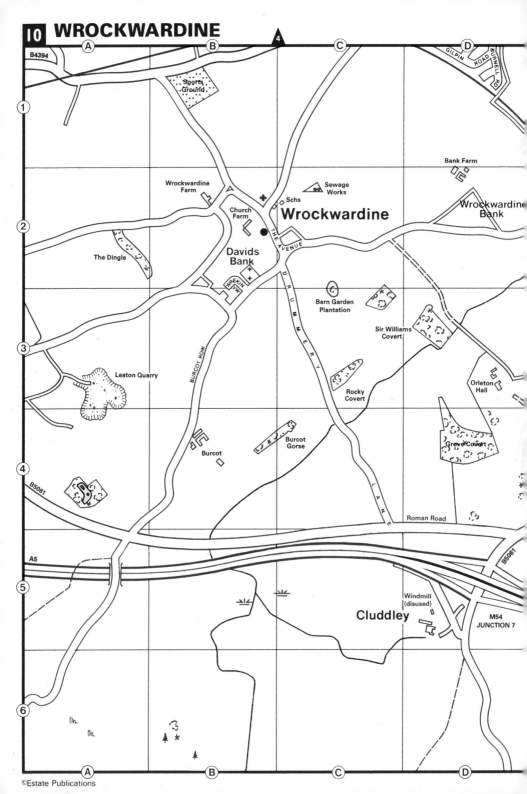

B4394

Sports Ground

Wrockwardine Farm

Wrockwardine

Schs

Sewage Works

Bank Farm

Church Farm

Wrockwardine Bank

Davids Bank

The Dingle

THE AVENUE

DRUMMERY

Barn Garden Plantation

Sir Williams Covert

Orleton Hall

WREKIN VW

BURCOT ROW

Leaton Quarry

Rocky Covert

Grove Covert

Burcot

Burcot Gorse

LANE

B5061

A5

Roman Road

B5061

Windmill (disused)

Cluddley

M54 JUNCTION 7

GILPIN ROAD

BURNELL RD

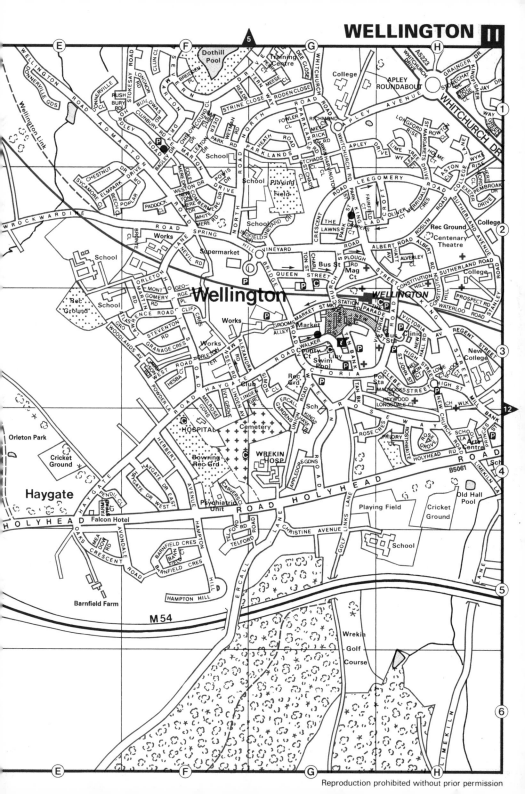

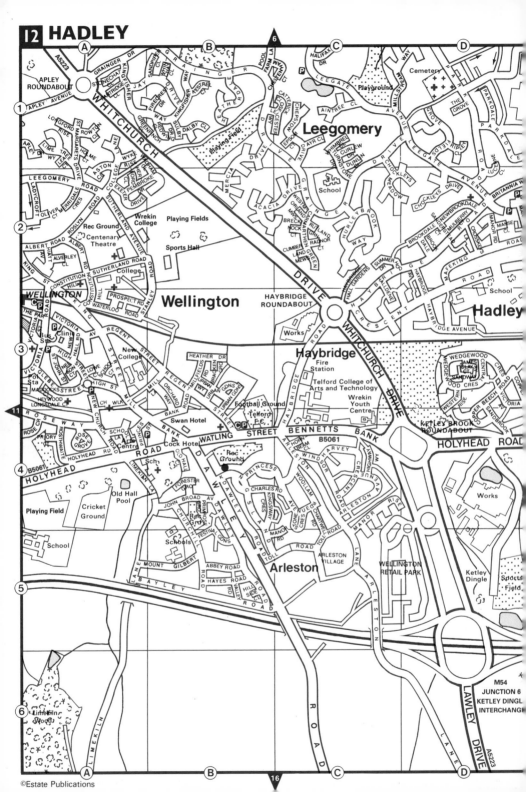

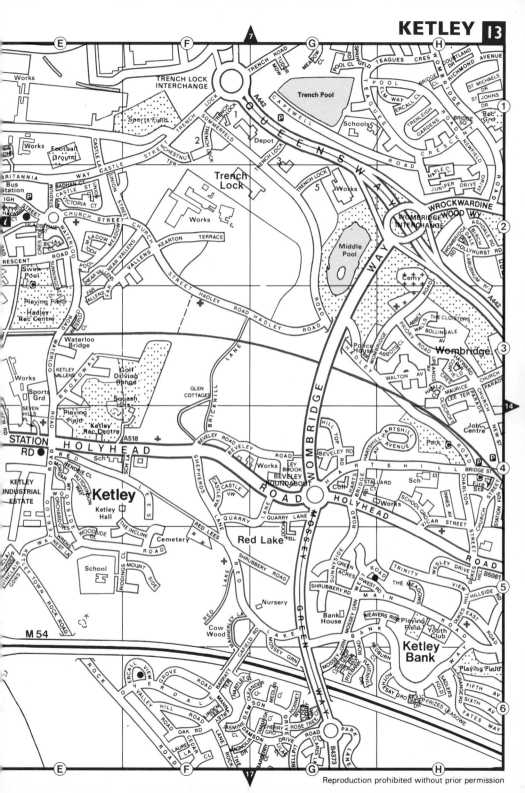

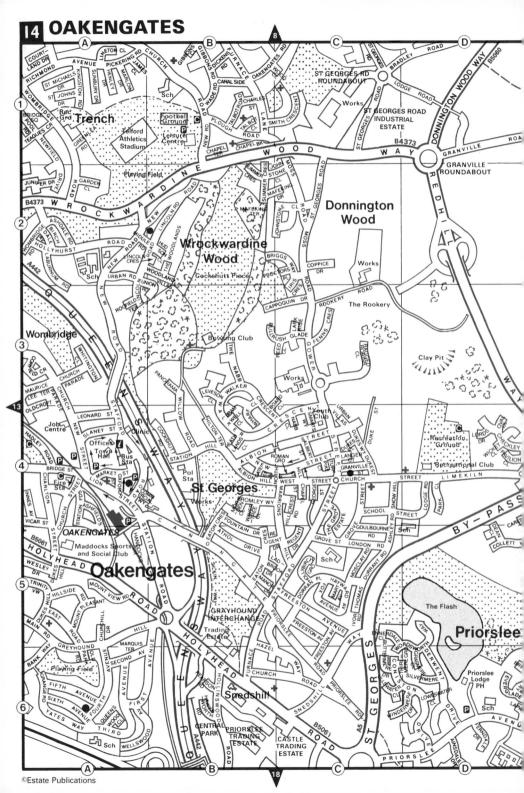

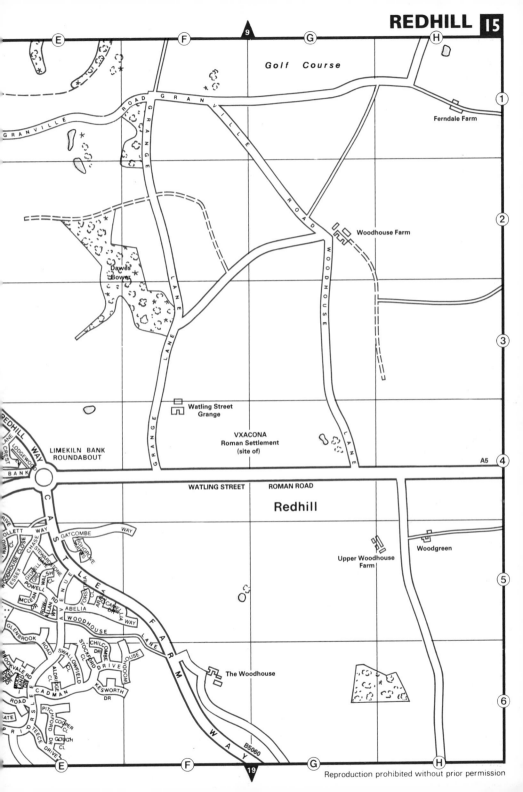

Golf Course

Ferndale Farm

GRANVILLE ROAD

GRANVILLE ROAD

GRANGE ROAD

WOODHOUSE ROAD

Woodhouse Farm

Dawes Bower

LANE

Watling Street Grange

VXACONA
Roman Settlement
(site of)

LIMEKILN BANK
ROUNDABOUT

REDHILL WAY

LODGEWOOD

CREST

BANK

GRANGE LANE

LANE

A5

WATLING STREET   ROMAN ROAD

Redhill

GATCOMBE WAY

CASTLE FARM LANE

OLLETT

ESSEX CLOSE

WOODHOUSE CLOSE

STEWART STONE

CHASE

GRENVILLE

WALSH

POWELL

McLEAN DR

BROWN RD

MORSE

ABELIA WAY

CAMELLIA WAY

CAMELLIA DR

WOODHOUSE LANE

GLENBROOK

CHILCOMBE DR

STOCKFORD CL

HOLLOM DRIVE

SWALLOWFIELD

ALDRIDGE CL

KESWORTH DR

CADMAN

BROOKVALE ROAD

PRIORSLEE ROAD

PITCHFORD DR

COOPER CL

TEECE DRIVE

GOUGH CL

Upper Woodhouse
Farm

Woodgreen

The Woodhouse

B5060

WAY

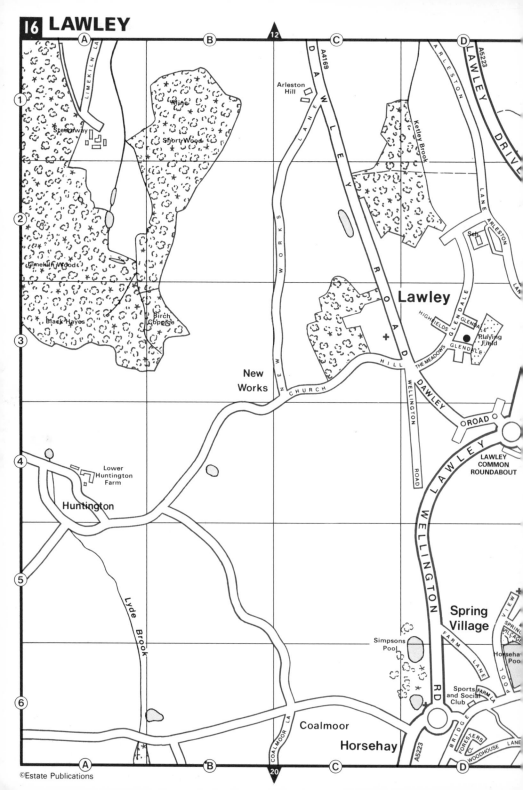

16 LAWLEY

Lawley

New Works

Huntington

Lower Huntington Farm

Spring Village

Coalmoor

Horsehay

LAWLEY COMMON ROUNDABOUT

Stennway

Short Wood

Mine

Arleston Hill

Limekiln Wood

Black Hayes

Birch Coppice

Playing Field

Simpsons Pool

Sports and Social Club

Lyde Brook

Ketley Brook

LIMEKILN LA

DAWLEY LANE

A4169

A5223

LAWLEY DRIVE

ARLESTON LANE

NEW WORKS LANE

CHURCH ROAD

DAWLEY ROAD

HILL

WELLINGTON ROAD

WELLINGTON ROAD

THE MEADOWS

HIGHFIELDS

GLENDALE

COALMOOR LA

FARM LANE

SPRING VILLAGE

Horsehay Pool

BRIDGE RD

FORESTERS

WOODHOUSE LANE

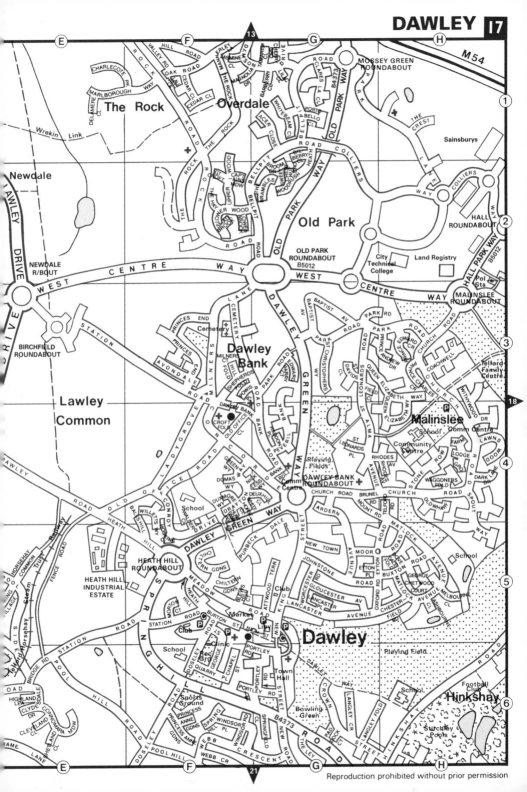

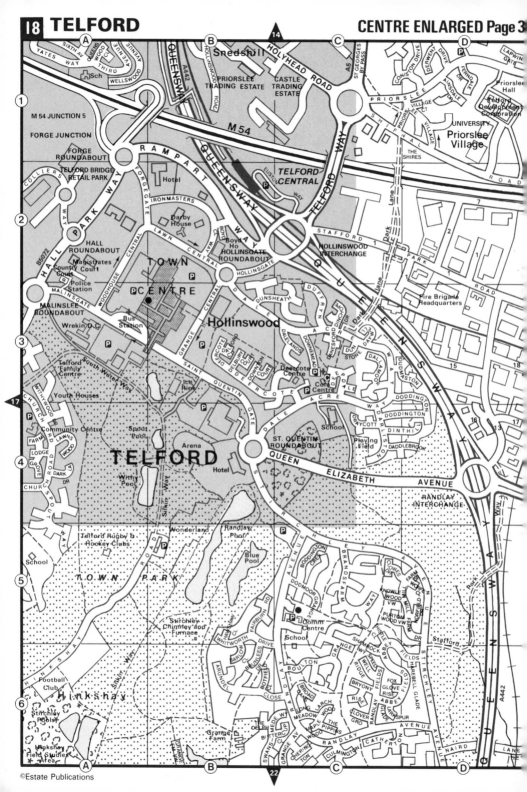

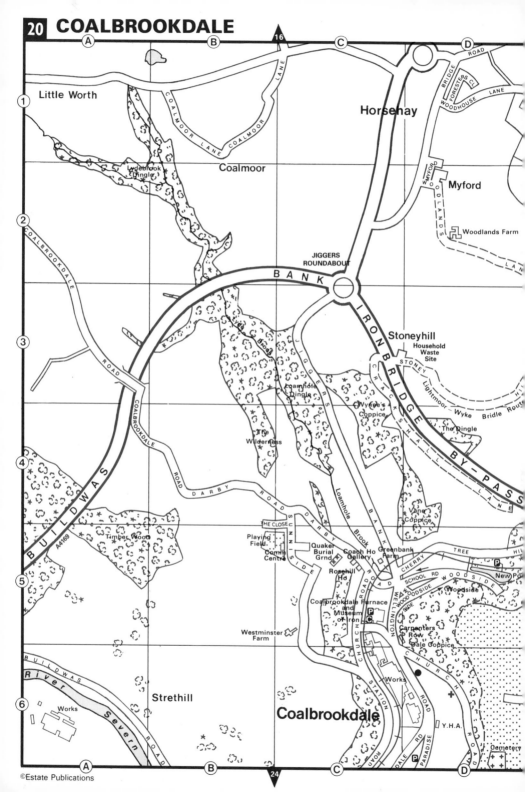

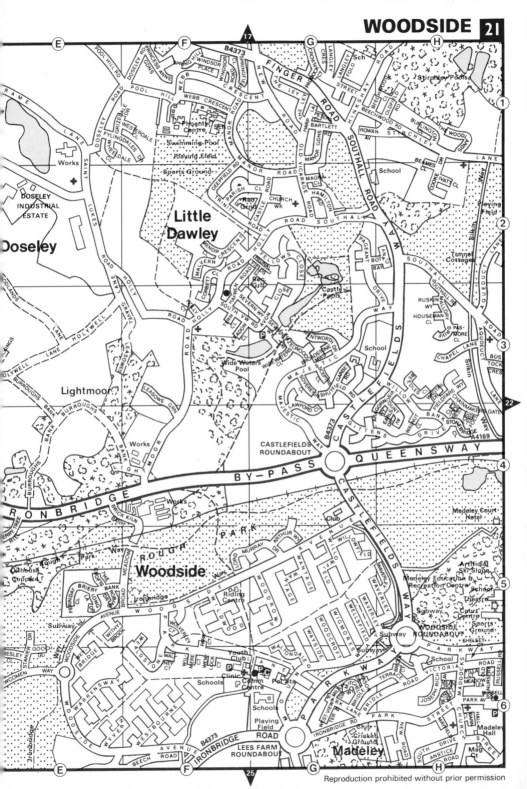

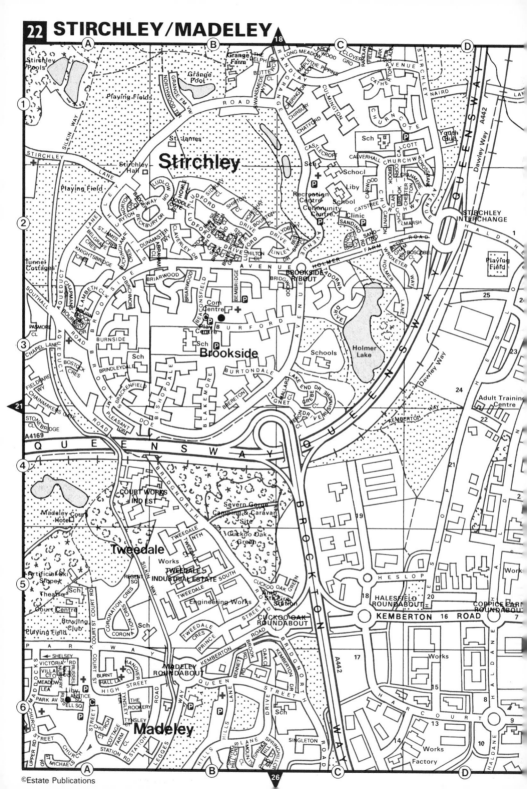

The Wyke

The Upper Wyke Farm

The Lower Wyke Farm

The Middle Wyke Farm

Doderoors

Old Mill Pond

The Hem Farm

Fish Pond

Hem Manor Farm

The Hem

Halesfield

5

6

Paddock Lane

4

5

Evelith Lane

Kemberton

Nursery

ctory

A4169

EMBERTON ROAD

West Ridge

HALL

LANE

Church Farm

GRINDLE ROAD

MILL LANE

B4379

Clews Wood

Works

A4169

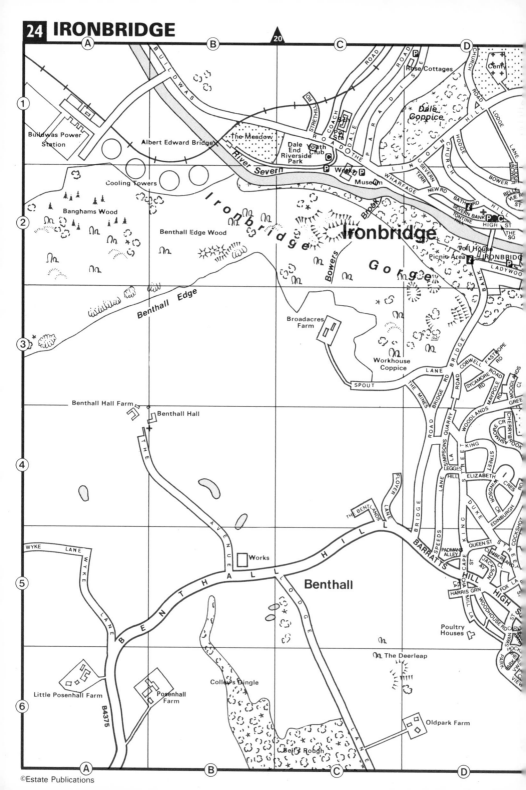

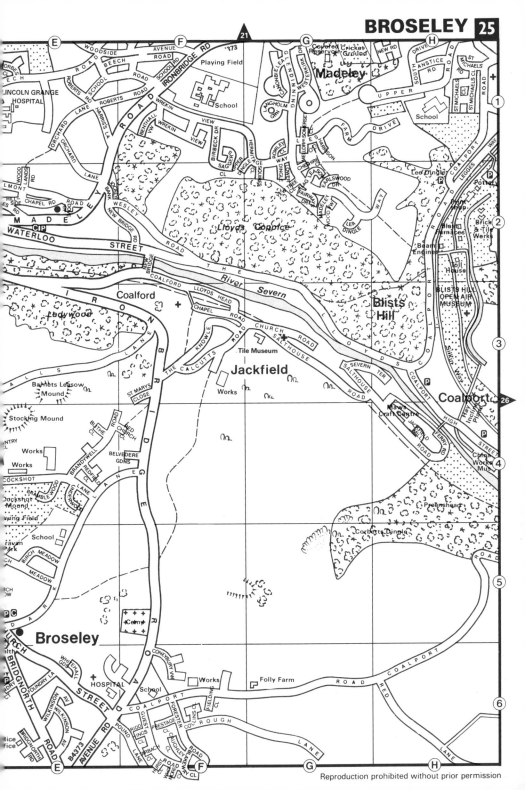

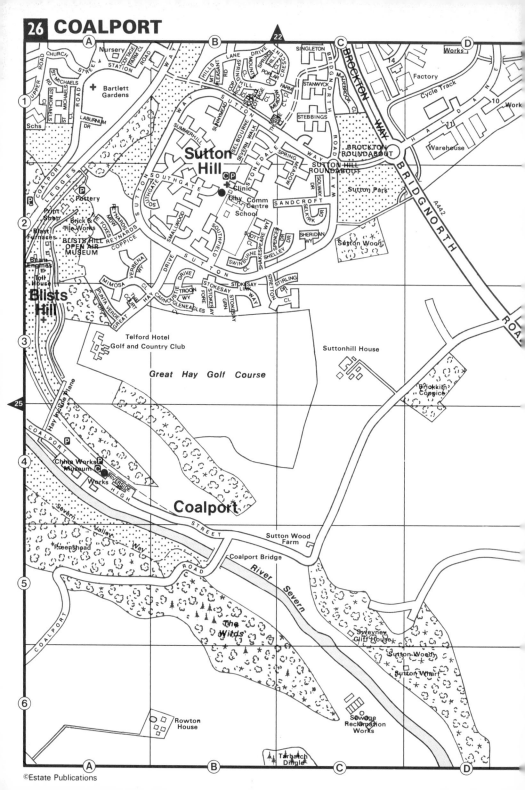

A - Z INDEX TO STREETS
with Postcodes

The Index includes some names for which there is insufficient space on the maps. These names are preceded by an * and are followed by the nearest adjoining thoroughfare.

TELFORD

Abbey Fields. TF3	18 C6
Abbey Rd. TF1	12 B5
Abbey Walls. TF2	13 H3
Abbots Clo. TF2	13 H3
Abelia Way. TF2	15 E5
Abraham Clo. TF3	22 B2
Acacia Dri. TF1	12 B2
Acer Clo. TF3	17 G1
Acorn Way. TF5	5 F5
Addison Rd. TF1	11 F3
Admaston Rd. TF1	11 E1
Admaston Spa. TF5	5 E5
Ainsdale Dri. TF2	18 D1
Aintree Clo. TF1	12 C1
Albacore Rd. TF1	6 C5
Albert Pl. TF2	8 C4
Albert Rd. TF1	11 H2
Albert St. TF2	14 C4
Albion Hill. TF2	14 B4
Albion St. TF2	14 B4
Alder Mead Clo. TF5	4 D5
Aldridge Clo. TF2	15 E6
Alexandra Rd. TF1	11 F3
Allertons Meadow. TF5	5 E4
Alma Av. TF4	17 G4
Almond Clo. TF2	8 D4
Alverley Clo. TF1	11 H2
Ambleside Way. TF2	8 D6
Andreas Dri. TF2	9 E4
Anson Dri. TF1	6 C6
Anstice Rd. TF7	25 H1
Anstice Sq. TF7	22 A6
Apley Av. TF1	11 G1
Apley Ct. TF1	5 G6
Apley Dri. TF1	11 G1
Appledore Gdns. TF1	11 G4
Aqueduct La. TF3	22 A3
Aqueduct Rd. TF3	22 A3
Aragorn Way. TF4	21 G4
Ardern Av. TF4	17 G4
Argyll Cres. TF2	8 D3
Arleston Av. TF1	12 C4
Arleston La. TF1	12 C4
Arleston Village. TF1	12 C5
Arran Way. TF2	9 E3
Arrow Rd. TF5	5 F3
Arthur Way. TF7	21 G5
Arundel Clo. TF3	18 B6
Ash Rd. TF2	8 D4
Ash-Lea Dri. TF2	8 C6
Ashbourne Clo. TF4	17 H5
Ashdale Rd. TF2	14 A2
Ashfields. TF2	14 A4
Ashley Rd. TF4	14 C5
Ashmore Cres. TF12	24 D4
Ashmore Dri. TF2	8 A6
Aspen Way. TF5	5 F4
Aston Clo. TF2	12 A1
Athol Dri. TF2	14 B5
Atlas Gro. TF1	11 F3
Attingham Clo. TF3	22 C2
Attwood Ter. TF4	17 G5
Auster Clo. TF1	6 C5

Avenue Rd. TF12	25 E6
Avon Clo. TF4	21 G3
Avondale. TF4	17 F3
Avondale Rd. TF1	11 F5
Ayr Clo. TF1	12 C1
Azalia Clo. TF2	15 E5
Bader Clo. TF1	6 C5
Badger Clo. TF3	22 A2
Badham Ct. TF1	13 E2
Bagley Dri. TF1	11 F1
Baldwin Webb Av. TF1	8 C4
Balls La. TF8	25 E3
Ballshill. TF4	17 F5
Bank Rd, Dawley. TF4	17 G4
Bank Rd, Wellington. TF1	12 B4
Bank Way. TF2	13 G5
Baptist Av. TF4	17 G3
Barber St. TF12	24 D5
Barberry Clo. TF3	13 G6
Barclay Ct. TF2	8 B5
Barlow Clo. TF3	18 B6
Barn Clo. TF2	8 D6
Barnes Wallis Dri. TF1	6 C5
Barnet Clo. TF1	11 F1
Barnfield Cres. TF1	11 F5
Barratt Ter. TF3	13 F6
Barratts Hill. TF12	24 D5
Bartlett Rd. TF4	21 G1
Bath Rd. TF8	24 D2
Bayley Rd. TF1	12 A4
Beaconsfield. TF3	22 B3
Beames Clo. TF4	21 H1
Beaufort Clo. TF1	6 C5
Beckbury Dri. TF3	22 A2
Bedstone Clo. TF3	22 C2
Beech Clo. TF1	11 E2
Beech Rd. TF7	25 E1
Beechwood Clo. TF4	21 H1
Beechwood Rd. TF4	21 G1
Beedles Clo. TF4	21 H3
Belgrave Cres. TF3	22 A2
Bell St. TF1	11 G3
Belle Vue Rd. TF8	24 D2
Bellpit Rd. TF3	17 G1
Belmont Rd. TF8	25 E2
Belvedere Gdns. TF12	25 F4
Bembridge. TF3	22 B2
Bennett Rd. TF7	22 B6
Bennetts Bank. TF1	12 C4
Benthall Hill. TF12	24 A5
Benthall Vw. TF7	25 F1
Bentley Grn. TF5	5 E4
Berberis Rd. TF1	6 C5
Betnell Gro. TF7	21 H6
Bevan Clo. TF1	13 E2
Beveley Rd. TF2	13 F4
Bilberry Clo. TF3	17 G1
Birbeck Dri. TF7	25 F1
Birch Dale Av. TF1	14 A2
Birch Meadow. TF1	25 E5
Birch Row. TF12	25 E5
Birchmore. TF3	22 A3
Bishopdale. TF3	22 B3
Blacksmiths Dri. TF3	13 G6
Blackthorn Grn. TF5	5 E4
Blakemore. TF3	22 B4
Blakeway Clo. TF12	25 F6
Blenheim Rd. TF1	6 C5
Blews Hill Ct. TF4	17 F5
Blithe Clo. TF12	25 E4
Bloomsbury Ct. TF2	8 D3
Board Clo. TF2	14 B4
Boddington Cres. TF3	18 C5

Body Rd. TF2	8 C1
Bollingale Av. TF2	13 H3
Boningale Clo. TF3	22 B2
Boscobel Clo. TF3	22 D2
Bostock Cres. TF3	22 A3
Botany Bay Clo. TF4	21 H2
Botfield Clo. TF3	18 B6
Boulton Grange. TF3	18 C6
Bournbrook Gdns. TF3	22 A3
Bournside Dri. TF3	22 A3
Bourton Clo. TF3	22 B2
Boyd Clo. TF3	3 C3
Bracken Gro. TF1	12 B3
Brackenfield. TF3	22 A3
Bradley Ct. TF2	8 D6
Bradley Rd. TF2	8 C6
Bramble Wood. TF12	25 E4
Bramwell Clo. TF2	14 B4
Brandon Gro. TF1	6 C5
Brands Meadow. TF2	9 E4
Brandsfarm Way. TF3	18 C5
Brandywell Rd. TF12	25 E4
Bratton Rd. TF5	4 D5
Bream Clo. TF2	7 H6
Brecknock Ct. TF1	12 C2
Breidden Pl. TF1	5 F6
Brereton. TF3	22 B3
Briarwood. TF3	22 B2
Brick Kiln Bank. TF7	21 E4
Brick Kiln Way. TF2	8 D5
Brickhill La. TF7	13 F4
Bridge Bank. TF8	24 D3
Bridge Clo. TF2	13 H1
Bridge Rd, Benthall. TF12	24 D3
Bridge Rd, Horsehay. TF4	16 D6
Bridge Rd, Wellington. TF1	11 G2
Bridge Sq. TF2	13 H1
Bridge St. TF2	13 H4
Bridge Way. TF2	8 D3
Bridgewood. TF3	22 B2
Bridgnorth Rd, Broseley. TF12	25 E6
Bridgnorth Rd, Sutton Hill. TF7	26 C2
Bridgnorth Rd, Tweedale. TF7	22 B4
Bridle Ct. TF7	21 H6
Bridle Rd. TF7	21 G6
Bridle Ter. TF7	21 G6
Briery Bank. TF7	21 E5
Briggs Way. TF2	14 C2
Brindleydale. TF3	22 A3
Britannia Way. TF1	12 D2
Broad Meadow La. TF7	21 F5
Broad Oaks. TF3	18 C6
Broadway. TF1	13 E3
Broadway Av. TF2	8 A6
Brockton Way. TF7	22 C5
Bromley Way. TF2	14 B4
Bronte Clo. TF1	11 F2
Brook Meadow. TF5	5 E4
Brook Rd. TF7	22 B5
Brookdale. TF1	12 D2
Brooklands. TF2	8 D3
Brookside. TF2	8 D3
Brookside Av. TF3	22 A3
Brookvale Rd. TF2	15 E6
Broom Dri. TF3	17 G2
Broomfield Rd. TF5	4 C6
Broomhurst Way. TF2	9 E4
Brunel Rd. TF4	17 G4

Brunlees Dri. TF3	18 B6
Bryony Rise. TF3	18 C6
Bryony Way. TF2	14 D6
Buckingham Cres. TF3	22 A2
Buildwas Rd, Ironbridge. TF8	24 B1
Buildwas Rd, Wellington. TF1	11 F1
Bullrush Glade. TF2	14 B3
Burcot Row. TF6	10 B3
Burford. TF3	22 B3
Burleigh Clo. TF3	22 B2
Burlington Clo. TF4	21 H1
Burnell Rd. TF5	4 D6
Burnside. TF3	22 A3
Burnt Hall La. TF7	22 A6
Burroughs Bank. TF4	21 E3
*Burton Clo, Heath Hill. TF4	17 E4
Burton St. TF4	17 F5
Burtondale. TF3	22 B3
Bush Clo. TF1	5 F6
Bustock Clo. TF5	4 D5
Buttercup Clo. TF3	18 C6
Buttermere Dri. TF2	14 C6
Butts Rd. TF5	5 E4
Buxton Rd. TF4	17 H5
Cactus Dri. TF1	6 C5
Cadman Dri. TF2	15 E6
Calcott. TF3	22 C1
Calcutts Rd. TF8	25 F3
Calverhall. TF3	22 C1
Camellia Dri. TF2	15 E5
Campion Dri. TF2	8 D5
Canal Side. TF2	14 B1
Canonbie Lee. TF7	25 G1
Canongate. TF2	14 B4
Cape St. TF12	24 D5
Capewell Rd. TF2	13 G1
Cappoquin Dri. TF2	14 C3
Captains Meadow. TF3	17 F2
Carlton Dri. TF2	14 D4
Carmarthen Grn. TF1	12 C2
Carnoustie Dri. TF7	26 B3
Carvers Clo. TF1	11 F4
Carvers Rd. TF12	24 D5
Carwood. TF3	22 C2
Castle Farm Way. TF2	15 E4
Castle La. TF1	13 E1
Castle Rd. TF4	21 G2
Castle St. TF1	13 E2
Castle View. TF1	13 F4
Castlecroft. TF3	22 C1
Castlefields Way. TF7	21 G4
Catherton. TF3	22 C1
Catstree. TF3	22 C2
Catterick Clo. TF1	12 C1
Caughley Clo. TF12	25 F6
Cavell Clo. TF1	6 B6
Caynton. TF3	22 C2
Cedar Clo. TF3	17 F1
Celandine Way. TF2	8 D5
Cemetery Rd. TF4	17 F3
Central Av. TF1	12 D3
Chainmakers Gate. TF2	21 H3
Chantry Clo. TF12	25 E4
Chapel Bank. TF2	14 B1
Chapel La, Broseley. TF12	24 D5
Chapel La, Woodside. TF3	21 H3
Chapel Rd, Ironbridge. TF8	25 E2

27

Chapel Rd, Jackfield.TF8 25 F3
Chapel St, Dawley. TF4 17 F6
Chapel St,
 St Georges. TF2 14 C4
Chapel Ter. TF2 14 B1
Chapmans Clo. TF3 22 A3
Charlecote Park. TF3 17 E1
Charles Rd. TF1 12 B4
Charles St. TF2 14 B1
Charlton St,
 Oakengates. TF2 13 H4
Charlton St,
 Wellington. TF1 11 G2
Chartwell Rd. TF1 12 C4
Chatford. TF3 22 C1
Checkley La. TF2 14 D4
Chelmarsh. TF3 22 C2
Cheltenham Clo. TF1 6 C6
Chepstow Dri. TF1 12 C1
Cherington. TF3 22 C1
Cherry Gro. TF3 13 G6
Cherry Tree Hill. TF8 20 D5
Cherrybrook Dri. TF12 24 D4
Cheshire Clo. TF7 25 G2
Cheshire Coppice La. TF5 4 C4
Chesterfield Rd. TF4 17 H5
Chesterton. TF3 22 D2
Chestnut Dri, Trench. TF2 7 H6
Chestnut Dri,
 Wellington. TF1 11 E2
Chestnut Ter. TF1 13 F1
Chetwynd Clo. TF3 22 B2
Chichester Dri. TF1 6 C5
Chilcombe Dri. TF2 15 E6
Chiltern Gdns. TF4 17 F5
Chirbury. TF3 22 C1
Chiswick Ct. TF2 8 D3
Chockleys Dri. TF1 12 D2
Chockleys Meadow. TF1 12 C2
Christine Av. TF1 11 G4
Church Ct. TF7 22 A6
Church Hill,
 Ironbridge. TF8 24 D1
Church Hill, Lawley. TF6 16 C3
Church Meadow. TF10 9 G1
Church Par. TF2 14 A3
Church Rd,
 Coalbrookdale. TF8 20 D6
Church Rd, Dawley. TF4 17 G4
Church Rd,
 Donnington. TF2 8 D5
Church Rd, Lilleshall. TF10 9 F2
Church Rd, Snedshill. TF2 14 B6
Church Rd, Trench. TF2 8 A6
Church St, Broseley. TF12 25 E5
Church St, Hadley. TF1 13 E2
Church St, Madeley. TF7 21 H6
Church St,
 Oakengates. TF2 14 A4
Church St,
 St Georges. TF2 14 C4
Church St,
 Wellington. TF1 11 G2
Church Walk,
 Donnington. TF2 8 C4
Church Walk,
 Little Dawley. TF4 21 G2
Church Walk,
 Wellington. TF1 11 H3
Churchill Dri. TF2 14 A5
Churchill Rd. TF1 12 B4
Churchward Clo. TF2 15 E5
Churchway. TF3 22 C2
Churncote. TF3 22 C1
Clanbrook. TF3 22 C2
Clares La. TF3 13 G6
Clares Lane Clo. TF3 17 G1
Claverley Dri. TF3 22 B2
*Clee Ct, Breidden Pl. TF1 5 F6

Clematis Dri. TF1 6 C5
Cleveland Clo. TF4 17 E6
Clift Cres. TF1 11 F3
Clover Gro. TF3 18 C6
*Clowes Dri, Knowle
 Wood View. TF3 18 C5
Clun Clo. TF1 5 F6
Clunbury Rd. TF1 11 F1
Clydesdale Dri. TF4 17 E6
Coach Central. TF3 3 B4
Coach Rd. TF8 24 C1
Coachman Meadow. TF1 5 F5
Coachwell Clo. TF3 3 A4
Coalbrookdale Rd. TF8 20 A2
Coalford. TF8 25 F2
Coalmoor La. TF4 20 B1
Coalport High St. TF8 26 A4
Coalport Rd,
 Broseley. TF12 25 F6
Coalport Rd,
 Coalport. TF7 25 H3
Cobwell Rd. TF12 24 D3
Cockshot La. TF12 24 D5
Cockshutt Rd. TF2 14 B4
Colemere Dri. TF1 11 F2
College La. TF1 12 A2
Collett Way. TF2 14 D5
Colliers Way. TF3 3 A2
Collins Clo. TF12 25 F6
Columbine Way. TF2 8 D5
Combermere Dri. TF1 11 F2
Commercial Way. TF2 14 A4
Concorde. TF1
Coney Green Way. TF1 5 G5
Coneybury Vw. TF12 25 F6
Coniston Dri. TF2 14 C6
Connemara Mdw. TF4 17 E6
Conroy Dri. TF4 17 F4
Constitution Hill. TF1 11 H2
Cooke Dri. TF4 21 H2
Cooper Clo. TF2 15 E6
Copper Beech Rd. TF1 12 D3
Copperfield Dri. TF2 8 D4
Coppice Clo. TF7 26 B1
Coppice Dri. TF6 14 C2
Corbett Clo. TF4 21 F3
Cordingley Way. TF2 8 B6
Corfield Cres. TF3 13 H3
Cornbrook. TF3 22 C2
Coronation Cres. TF7 22 A5
Coronation Dri. TF2 8 D4
Cote Rd. TF5 5 E4
Cottage Clo. TF7 26 B1
Cottage Farm Clo. TF7 22 A6
Cound Clo. TF1 11 F1
Court Rd. TF7 22 A5
Court St. TF7 22 A5
Courtland Dri. TF2 8 A6
Cranage Cres. TF1 11 F3
Cranmere. TF3 22 D2
Crescent Rd, Hadley. TF1 12 C3
Crescent Rd,
 Wellington. TF1 11 G2
Crest Rd. TF2 15 E4
Cricketers La. TF2 14 D4
Croft Fold. TF4 17 F4
Crossbank. TF3 22 D1
Crosskeys La. TF1 12 D2
Crowdale Rd. TF5 5 E4
Crown St, Dawley. TF4 17 G6
Crown St,
 Wellington. TF1 11 G3
Cuckoo Oak Green.TF7 22 B5
Cuckoos Rest. TF4 21 H4
Culmington. TF3 22 C1
Cumberland Clo. TF12 24 D5
Cumberland Mews. TF1 11 G2
Curie Croft. TF1 6 B6
Curlew Dri. TF1 12 C1

Cygnet Dri. TF3 22 C3
Cyril Hayward Ct. TF1 13 E2
Daddlebrook. TF3 18 C4
Dalby Clo. TF1 12 B1
Dale Acre Way. TF3 3 C4
Dale Rd. TF8 24 C1
Dalelands. TF3 3 D4
Dalford Ct. TF3 3 C4
Dallamoor. TF3 18 C3
Damson Dri. TF3 13 G6
Danesford. TF3 3 D4
Darby Rd. TF8 20 B4
Dark La. TF3 25 E5
Dark Lane Dri. TF3 3 A6
Darliston. TF3 18 C4
Darwin Rd. TF1 11 G1
Dawley Bank. TF4 17 F4
Dawley Green Way. TF4 17 G3
Dawley Rd. TF1 12 B4
Dawley Way. TF4 17 G6
Daywell. TF3 18 C3
Dean Clo. TF2 14 D5
Dee Clo. TF1 5 G6
Deepdale. TF3 3 D5
Deepfield Rd. TF4 21 F2
Deer Park Rd. TF1 11 F1
Deercote. TF3 3 C4
Delamere Clo. TF3 17 E1
Delbury Ct. TF3 3 C4
Delphside. TF12 25 E5
Derwent Dri. TF2 14 D6
Deuxhill Clo. TF4 17 G4
Dickens Rd. TF2 8 B6
Dinchope Dri. TF3 3 D4
Dinthill. TF3 18 C4
Doddington. TF3 18 C4
Doddlecote Clo. TF3 22 B2
Dodmoor Grange. TF3 18 C5
Domas Way. TF4 17 F4
Donnerville Clo. TF1 11 E1
Donnerville Gdns. TF5 11 E1
Donnington Dri. TF2 8 B1
Donnington Way. TF2 8 C2
Donnington Wood
 Way. TF2 8 D4
Dorran Pl. TF2 14 C5
Doseley Rd. TF4 21 E1
*Dothill Ct,
 Breidden Pl. TF1 5 F6
Dove Ct. TF8 25 E2
Dovedale Fold. TF4 17 H5
Downemead. TF3 3 D4
Downton Court. TF3 3 C5
Drapers Ct. TF1 11 G2
Draycott. TF3 3 D5
Drayton Way. TF4 17 F4
Drummery La. TF6 10 C2
Dudmaston. TF3 18 D3
Duffryn. TF3 3 D4
Duke St, Broseley. TF12 24 D4
Duke St, St Georges. TF2 14 C4
Duke St, Wellington. TF1 11 G3
Dukes Hill. TF2 14 A5
Dukes Pl. TF2 14 C4
Dukes Way. TF2 14 C4
Dunlin Clo. TF1 12 C1
Dunmaster Way. TF3 22 A2
Dunsheath. TF3 3 C4
Dunstone. TF3 3 D4
Durrant Rd. TF2 14 C5
Duxmore Way. TF4 17 F4

Earls Dri. TF4 21 H4
Earlswood Dri. TF7 25 G2
East Av. TF2 8 B5
East Rd. TF2 14 A5
Easthope Rd. TF12 24 D3
Eaton Cres. TF2 14 B5

Edinburgh Rd. TF12 24 D4
Edward Parry Ct. TF4 17 G3
Eglantine Clo. TF2 9 E4
Eider Dri. TF1 6 B5
Elderberry Clo. TF3 13 G6
Elizabeth Cres. TF12 24 D4
Elm Way. TF2 13 H1
Elmpark Dri. TF1 11 E2
Elmsdale Cres. TF5 4 D5
Emral Rise. TF1 5 G6
Ennerdale Clo. TF2 14 C5
Epsom Ct. TF1 12 C1
Ercall Clo. TF2 13 H1
Ercall Gdns. TF1 11 G3
Ercall La. TF1 11 F5
Ercall View. TF3 13 F6
Essex Chase. TF2 15 E5
Euston Way. TF3 3 C2
Evelith La. TF11 23 H5
Everglade Rd. TF2 14 D6
Ewart Rd. TF2 8 C6
Exeter Dri. TF1 12 A2
Eyton Pl. TF4 17 G5
Eyton Rd. TF4 17 G5
Eyton View. TF1 5 G6
Fairburn Rd. TF3 18 B5
Fairfield Clo. TF2 11 G2
Fairways Dri. TF7 25 G2
Fallow Rd. TF5 5 E4
Far Vallens. TF1 13 E3
Farm Clo. TF7 26 C1
Farm La. TF4 16 D5
Farm Lane Bungalows. TF2 8 C5
Farm Lodge Gro. TF3 3 A5
Farmstead Ct. TF1 11 E4
Fellows Clo. TF4 21 G2
Fence Rd. TF4 17 E5
Fenns Cres. TF2 14 C3
Ferndale Dri. TF2 18 D1
Fernwood Clo. TF1 5 G5
Ferriday Clo. TF7 21 E5
Ferry Rd. TF8 25 H4
Festival Gdns. TF1 12 B4
Field Clo. TF4 17 G3
Field House Dri. TF2 8 D3
Field Rd. TF2 8 A5
Fieldfare Way. TF4 21 H4
Fielding Clo. TF12 25 F6
Fifth Av. TF2 14 A6
Finger Rd. TF4 21 G1
Firecrest Dri. TF1 12 B1
First Av. TF2 14 A6
Flag Leasow. TF7 25 G2
Fleming Ct. TF1 6 B6
Floyer La. TF12 24 C4
Forest Clo. TF5 5 F4
Forester Gro. TF1 12 B4
Forester Rd. TF12 25 F6
Foresters Clo. TF4 16 D6
Forgegate. TF3 3 B2
Forsythia Clo. TF2 15 E5
Fosters Foel. TF4 21 H4
Foundry Clo. TF12 25 E6
Foundry La. TF12 25 E6
Fountain Dri. TF2 14 B5
Fourth Av. TF2 14 A6
Fowler Clo. TF1 11 G1
Fox Av. TF2 14 C5
Fox La. TF3 24 D5
Foxes Covert. TF5 5 E4
Foxglove Rise. TF3 18 C6
Frame La. TF4 21 E1
Freeston Av. TF4 14 C5
Frizes Leasowe. TF2 13 H6
Furnace La. TF8 8 B5
Furnace Rd. TF2 14 B6
Fylingdales Dri. TF4 21 E1

Street	Ref
Gafield Rd. TF3	13 F6
Garbet Rd. TF4	21 G3
Garden Clo. TF2	14 A2
Gatcombe Way. TF2	15 E5
Gate St. TF2	14 B4
George Chetwood Ct. TF4	17 H5
George Pl. TF1	11 F2
George St, Dawley. TF4	17 F6
George St, St Georges. TF2	14 C4
Gibbons Clo. TF2	8 B6
Gibbons Rd. TF2	8 B5
Gilpin Rd. TF5	4 D6
Gilwell Gro. TF2	15 E5
Gittens Dri. TF4	21 G4
Glade Way. TF5	5 E4
Gladstone St. TF1	13 E2
Glebe St. TF1	11 H3
Glebelands. TF2	8 C5
Glen Cotts. TF2	13 F3
Glenbrook Rd. TF2	15 E5
Glendale. TF4	16 D3
Glendinning Way. TF7	25 G1
Gleneagles Clo. TF7	26 B3
Gloucester Av. TF4	17 G5
Gloucester Ct. TF1	6 C5
Glovers Way. TF5	4 D4
Golf Links La. TF1	11 G5
Gooch Clo. TF7	21 E6
Goodyear Way. TF2	8 D5
Gordon Rd. TF2	8 A6
Gough Clo. TF2	15 E6
Goulbourne Rd. TF2	14 C5
Gower Clo. TF2	9 E3
Gower St. TF2	14 C3
Grainger Dri. TF1	12 B1
Grampian Clo. TF2	9 E3
Grange Av. TF3	22 C1
Grange Central. TF3	3 C4
Grange La. TF2	15 F1
Grange Rd. TF2	14 A6
Granville Dri. TF2	9 E4
Granville Rd. TF2	14 D1
Granville St. TF2	14 C4
Grasmere Clo. TF2	14 D6
Gravel Leasowes. TF4	21 F3
Great Croft. TF3	17 F2
Great Hay Dri. TF7	26 A3
Grebe Clo. TF3	22 C3
Green Acres. TF2	13 G5
Green Way. TF4	17 F4
Greenaway Pl. TF2	8 B6
Greenfinch Clo. TF1	12 A1
Greengage Way. TF2	8 D4
Greenlea Rd. TF2	14 A1
Gresley Clo. TF7	21 E6
Greyhound Hill. TF2	14 A5
Grindle Rd. TF11	23 G6
Grinshill Flats. TF1	5 F6
Grizedale Dri. TF4	21 E1
Groom Alley. TF1	11 G3
Grove Fields. TF1	12 D1
Grove Rd. TF3	13 F6
Grove St. TF2	14 C5
Guest Rd. TF12	25 F6
Guests Clo. TF7	8 D5
Guisbourne Av. TF5	5 F4
Haddon Pl. TF4	17 G4
Hadley Gdns. TF1	6 C5
Hadley Park Rd. TF1	6 C5
Hadley Rd. TF2	13 F3
Hafren Rd. TF4	21 F3
Halcyon Ct. TF2	9 E4
Haldane. TF2	22 D2
Halifax Dri. TF1	6 C6
Hall Barn Clo. TF7	21 H6
Hall La. TF11	23 F6
Hall Park Way. TF3	3 A3
Halldene. TF1	12 C2
Hamilton Rd. TF4	21 G2
Hamlet Clo. TF2	13 H3
Hampton Hill. TF1	11 F5
Hancocks Dri. TF1	14 A5
Hanover Ct. TF7	22 A6
Harcourt. TF7	22 C6
Harebell Glade. TF3	18 D6
Harley Clo. TF1	5 F5
Harp La. TF4	21 G1
Harrington Heath. TF5	5 E4
Harris Grn. TF12	24 D5
Harris's La. TF8	25 E1
Harrison Clo. TF7	25 G1
Hartley Clo. TF3	13 F6
Hartsbridge Rd. TF2	13 G4
Hartshill. TF2	13 G4
Hartshill Av. TF2	13 G4
*Hartshorn Ct, Meadow Rd. TF4	17 F5
Harvey Cres. TF1	12 C4
Harvington Clo. TF1	11 G1
Haughmond Ct. TF1	5 G6
Haughton Rd. TF11	19 G2
Hawksworth Rd. TF2	14 B6
Hawshaw Clo. TF3	18 B5
Hawthorn Pl. TF2	8 C4
Hawthorn Rd. TF2	8 C5
Haybridge Av. TF1	12 D2
Haybridge Hall Gdns. TF1	12 C2
Haybridge Rd. TF1	12 C3
Haybrook. TF7	23 E6
Haycocks Clo. TF1	5 F6
Hayes Rd. TF1	12 B5
Haygate Dri East. TF1	11 F4
Haygate Dri West. TF1	11 F4
Haygate Rd. TF1	11 E4
Hayward Av, Donnington. TF2	8 C5
Hayward Av, St Georges. TF2	14 C5
Hayward Par. TF2	13 H3
Hazel Way. TF2	14 B6
Hazelwood Dri. TF4	21 G3
Heath Hill. TF4	17 E4
Heath Rd. TF1	11 G1
Heather Dri. TF1	12 B3
Heatherdale. TF1	12 B1
Heathlands Clo. TF1	14 B4
Hem La. TF7	23 E3
Hendrie Clo. TF1	13 E4
Henley Dri. TF2	8 A6
Herbert Av. TF1	11 F4
Hermitage Way. TF7	25 G1
Heron Clo. TF3	22 C4
Hertford Clo. TF1	12 A2
Hesba Clo. TF1	11 F3
Heslop. TF7	22 D3
Heywood Longdale Ct. TF1	11 H3
Hiatt Av. TF1	11 H2
High Mount. TF2	8 C6
High St, Broseley. TF12	24 D5
High St, Dawley. TF4	17 F5
High St, Hadley. TF1	13 E2
High St, Ironbridge. TF8	24 D2
High St, Madeley. TF7	22 A6
High St, Wellington. TF1	11 H3
Highfields. TF4	16 D3
Highgrove Mdws. TF2	15 E5
Highland Lea. TF4	17 E6
Highway Way. TF1	12 C4
Hilda Hooke Clo. TF7	26 B1
Hill Crest Rd. TF1	14 C4
Hill Fold. TF4	17 F3
Hill Rd, Donnington. TF2	8 C1
Hill Rd, Overdale. TF2	13 F6
Hill St. TF1	14 C4
Hill Top Rd. TF2	13 G4
Hills Lane. TF7	22 B6
Hills Lane Dri. TF7	22 B6
Hillside. TF8	25 E2
Hillside Clo. TF1	12 B5
Hillside E. TF10	9 G1
Hillside Rd. TF2	14 A5
Hilton Clo. TF3	22 B2
Hilton Ter. TF2	14 B4
Hinkshay Rd. TF4	17 H6
Hockley Rd. TF12	24 D6
Hodge Bower. TF8	24 D1
Holland Dri. TF2	9 E4
Hollies Rd. TF1	11 F2
Hollinsgate. TF3	3 C3
Hollinswood Rd. TF2	3 C1
Holly Rd. TF4	21 F2
Hollybirch Gro.TF2	14 C5
Hollyhurst Rd. TF2	14 A2
Holme Ct. TF1	12 A1
Holmer Farm Rd. TF3	22 C2
Holmer La. TF3	22 C2
Holyhead Rd, Oakengates. TF2	3 D1
Holyhead Rd, Wellington. TF1	11 E4
Holywell La. TF4	21 E3
Hopeshay Clo. TF3	22 B2
Hopkins Heath. TF5	5 E4
Hordley Rd. TF1	11 F1
Hornbeam Clo. TF1	12 C4
Horne Rd. TF2	8 C1
Hornet Way. TF3	13 G6
Horse Chestnut Dri. TF5	5 F4
Horsehay Common. TF4	17 E5
Horton La, Horton. TF1	7 F2
Horton La, Trench. TF1	7 G6
Horton Rd. TF2	7 G6
Horton Wood. TF1	7 F5
Hoskins Clo. TF4	17 F5
Houseman Clo. TF3	21 H3
Howle Clo. TF3	22 B2
Hudson Clo. TF2	14 B2
Humber La. TF2	8 A1
Humber Way. TF2	8 A2
Huntsman Way. TF4	17 F4
Hurleybrook Way. TF1	12 C2
Hurst Clo. TF12	25 F6
Hutchinson Way. TF1	13 E4
Hyde Clo. TF2	9 E4

INDUSTRIAL ESTATES:

Estate	Ref
Castle Trading Est. TF2	3 C1
Central Park. TF2	14 B6
Heath Hill Ind Est. TF4	17 E5
Ketley Ind Est. TF1	13 E4
Priorslee Trading Est. TF2	3 C1
St Georges Rd Ind Est. TF2	14 C1
Telford Bri. Retail Park. TF3	3 A2
Innes Av. TF2	13 H4
Iris Cres. TF2	14 C2
Ironbridge By-Pass. TF4	20 C3
Ironbridge Rd, Broseley. TF12	25 E3
Ironbridge Rd, Madeley. TF7	21 F6
Ironmasters Way. TF3	3 B2
Ivatt Clo. TF4	21 H2
Ivor Thomas Rd. TF2	14 C5
Ivy Gro. TF1	11 F3
Jackson Av. TF12	24 D5
James Clay Ct. TF1	12 D3
James Clo. TF2	8 A6
James Nelson Cres. TF2	8 B5
James WayTF2	8 B5
Japonica. TF1	6 C5
Jasmine Clo. TF3	13 F6
Jay Dri. TF1	12 A1
Jiggers Bank. TF8	20 C3
Jockey Bank. TF8	25 E2
John Broad Av. TF1	12 B4
Johnstone Clo. TF2	14 C2
Johnstone Rd. TF4	17 G5
Joseph Rich Av. TF7	21 H6
Jubilee Av. TF2	8 C4
Juniper Dri. TF2	13 H2
Kearton Ter. TF1	13 F1
Kemberton Dri. TF7	22 C6
Kemberton Rd. TF7	22 C5
Kemberton Way. TF7	22 C4
Kestrel Ct. TF1	12 B1
Kesworth Dri. TF2	15 E6
Ketley Town. TF1	13 E5
Ketley Vallens. TF1	13 E3
King St, Broseley. TF12	24 D4
King St, Dawley. TF4	17 G5
King St, Wellington. TF1	11 G2
Kings Haye Rd. TF1	11 G4
Kingsland. TF1	12 B4
Kingsley Dri. TF2	8 C3
Kingston Rd. TF2	14 A1
Kingsway Cres. TF1	12 B4
Knightsbridge Cres. TF3	22 A2
Knowle Wood View. TF3	18 C5
Laburnum Dri. TF7	26 A1
Laburnum Rd. TF2	14 A2
Ladbrook Dri. TF2	14 B5
Ladycroft. TF1	11 G2
Ladygrove. TF4	17 F4
Ladywood. TF8	24 D2
Lambeth Dri. TF3	22 A3
Lancaster Av. TF4	17 G5
Lancaster Pl. TF4	17 G5
Landy Clo. TF2	8 C2
Laneside. TF2	9 E3
Langer Ct. TF2	14 C4
Langholm Grn. TF7	25 G1
Langley Cres. TF4	17 G6
Langley Fold. TF4	17 G6
Lapwing Gate. TF2	14 D6
Larch Wood. TF3	18 C6
Lark Rise. TF2	14 C3
Larkspur Glade. TF3	18 C6
Laurel La. TF3	13 F6
Lawford Clo. TF4	21 G4
Lawley Dri. TF2	12 D6
Lawn Central. TF3	3 B3
Lawndale. TF2	8 B5
Lawns Wood. TF3	3 A5
Lawrence Rd. TF1	11 F3
Lawton Farm Clo. TF1	6 C6
Lawton Farm Way. TF1	6 C6
Lea Ct. TF1	12 A1
Lea Dingle. TF1	25 G2
Leadon Clo. TF4	21 F3
Leaton Dri. TF1	11 F1
Leegate Av. TF1	6 C5
Leegomery Rd. TF1	11 G2
Lees Farm Dri. TF7	25 G1
Leeses Clo. TF5	5 E4
Legges Hill. TF12	24 D4
Legges Way. TF7	26 A2
Leicester Way. TF1	12 C1
Lennock Rd. TF2	8 B5
Leonard Clo. TF2	8 B5
Leonard St. TF2	14 A4
Leveson Clo. TF2	14 B3
Ley Brook. TF2	13 G4
Lhen Clo. TF2	9 E4
Lightmoor Rd. TF7	21 F4
Lilac Clo. TF3	13 G6
Lilyhurst Rd. TF10	9 F2
Lime Tree Way. TF1	12 A1

Limekiln Bank. TF2	14 D4	Marlow Dri. TF2	8 A6
Limekiln La. TF1	12 A4	Marquis Ter. TF2	14 A6
Lincoln Cres. TF2	14 A2	Marrions Hill. TF2	14 C4
Lincoln Hill. TF8	24 C2	Marsh Meadow Clo. TF1	5 F5
Lincoln Rd. TF2	14 A3	Marshbrook Way. TF2	9 E4
Linden Av. TF1	11 F3	Mart Av. TF2	14 C5
Linden Gro. TF1	11 F3	Martin Rd. TF1	11 F3
Linden Ter. TF1	13 F6	Marton Dri. TF1	11 F1
Lindfield Dri. TF1	11 F2	Mason Dri. TF7	21 G6
Lineton Clo. TF2	8 A6	Matlock Av. TF4	17 H5
Linley Dri. TF3	22 B2	Maurice Lee Av. TF2	13 H3
Lion St. TF2	14 A4	Mayfield. TF7	21 H6
Lloyds Head. TF8	25 F3	Maypole Rd. TF12	24 D3
Lodge La, Benthall. TF12	24 C5	Mead Croft. TF2	21 H6
Lodge La, Ironbridge. TF8	24 D1	Meadow Clo, Madeley. TF7	26 B1
Lodge Rd, Donnington. TF2	14 C1	Meadow Clo, Trench. TF2	7 G6
Lodge Rd, St Georges. TF2	14 D4	Meadow Lea. TF7	22 A6
Lodgewood La. TF2	15 E4	Meadow Rd, Dawley. TF4	17 F5
London Rd. TF2	14 C5	Meadow Rd, Muxton. TF2	8 D4
Long Lane Dri. TF1	21 E5	Meadow Rd, Wellington. TF1	11 E5
Long Meadow. TF3	18 C6	Meadowsweet Dri. TF1	15 E6
Longford Rise. TF1	12 A1	Medlar Clo. TF3	13 G6
*Longmynd Ct, Breidden Pl. TF1	5 F6	Meese Clo. TF1	11 G1
Longnor Rd. TF1	11 F1	Melbourne Clo. TF4	17 H5
Lord Murray Dri. TF7	21 G5	Mellor Clo. TF7	25 G1
Lords Dri. TF2	14 D4	Melrose Gdns. TF1	11 F3
Lowe Ct. TF1	11 H3	Mendip Clo. TF4	21 F2
Lower Brook. TF3	17 F2	Mercia Dri. TF1	12 B2
Lower Dingle. TF7	25 G2	Mere Gro. TF5	5 F4
Lower Park Dri. TF1	5 F5	Merridale Cres. TF1	11 H2
Lower Wood. TF3	17 F2	Merrington Rd. TF2	9 E3
Loweswater Clo. TF2	14 D6	Meyrick Rd. TF1	11 G1
Lucerne Clo. TF1	12 D2	Middle Rd. TF2	14 A2
Ludford Dri. TF3	22 B2	Mill Bank. TF1	12 A3
Ludlow Dri. TF3	22 B2	Mill Farm Dri. TF3	18 D5
Lydbury Clo. TF3	22 C2	Mill La, Broseley. TF12	24 D5
Lyndhurst Dri. TF2	8 A6	Mill La, Kemberton. TF11	23 G6
		Mill La, Wellington. TF1	12 B3
		Mill Way. TF2	7 H6
McCormick Dri. TF1	5 F5	Millers Way. TF2	9 E4
McLean Dri. TF1	15 E5	Millfields Rd. TF1	12 B3
Maddocks. TF7	22 A6	Millstream Way. TF1	6 D6
Maddocks Ct. TF1	11 H3	Milners Ct. TF4	17 F3
Madebrook Clo. TF7	26 C1	Milners La. TF4	17 F3
Madeley Rd. TF8	25 E2	Milton Dri. TF7	21 G6
Madeley Wood Vw. TF7	25 G2	Milward Clo. TF2	8 B5
Mafeking Dri. TF2	14 C2	Mimosa Clo. TF7	26 A2
Mafeking Rd. TF1	12 D2	Mitchel Way. TF7	21 G6
Mafeking Ter. TF2	14 B2	Mole Way. TF5	5 F5
Magna Clo. TF4	21 G2	Montgomery Mws. TF1	6 C5
Magnolia Dri. TF3	13 F6	Montgomery Rd. TF1	11 F3
Main Rd. TF2	13 G5	Moor Rd. TF4	17 G5
Majestic Way. TF4	21 G3	Moorland Dri. TF2	15 E6
Malinsgate. TF3	3 A4	Morden Clo. TF2	14 B4
Mallory Dri. TF3	21 H3	Morgan Way. TF1	13 E4
Malvern Cres. TF4	21 F2	Morris Dri. TF2	8 C4
Manchester Dri. TF1	6 C5	Morville Dri. TF1	5 F6
Mannerley La. TF3	13 F6	Mosclay Rd. TF2	14 C5
Manor Dri. TF2	14 B5	Moss Rd. TF2	14 C2
Manor Gdns. TF4	21 G1	Mossey Green Way. TF1	13 G5
Manor Rise. TF1	12 C4	Mossey Grn. TF2	13 G5
Manor Road, Arleston. TF1	12 C5	Mound Way. TF7	21 G6
Manor Road, Hadley. TF1	12 D2	Mount Gilbert. TF1	12 B4
Manor Road, Little Dawley. TF4	21 F1	Mount Pleasant. TF1	14 A5
Manse Clo. TF1	12 D2	Mount Pleasant Dri. TF3	22 A4
Manse Rd. TF1	12 D2	Mount Pleasant Rd. TF7	26 B1
Mansell Rd. TF1	11 F3	Mount Rd. TF4	17 G4
Maple Clo. TF2	13 H2	Mount Side. TF1	13 F5
Maple Wood. TF3	18 C6	Mount View Rd. TF2	14 A5
Market Sq. TF1	11 G3	Mounts Clo. TF7	26 B1
Market St, Oakengates. TF2	14 A4	Mulberry Ct. TF1	12 D2
Market St, Wellington, TF1	11 G3	Mullinder Dri. TF2	13 H6
Marlborough Way. TF3	17 E1	Musk Rose Clo. TF2	8 D4
		Muxton La. TF2	9 E3
		Myford. TF4	20 D2
		Nabb Clo. TF2	14 C4

Naird La. TF3	18 D6	Park La. TF3	17 G1
Near Vallens. TF1	13 E2	Park Lane Av. TF7	21 G6
Nelson Ct. TF1	11 H3	Park Rd, Donnington. TF2	8 B6
Nelson Way. TF2	9 E3	Park Rd, Malinslee. TF4	17 G3
Nevil Rd. TF1	11 F2	Park St, Madeley. TF7	21 H6
New Bridge. TF8	25 F2	Park St, Wellington. TF1	11 G2
New Bridge Rd. TF8	25 E2	Park View. TF8	24 D6
New Church Rd. TF1	11 H4	Parkdale. TF1	12 D1
New Hall Rd. TF1	11 H3	Parklands. TF1	11 G1
New Rd, Donnington. TF2	8 C5	Parkway. TF7	21 G6
New Rd, Ironbridge. TF8	24 D2	Partridge Clo. TF1	12 A1
New Rd, Little Dawley. TF4	21 G1	Pasmore Clo. TF3	21 H3
New Rd, Madeley. TF7	21 H6	Pasteur Dri. TF1	6 B3
New Rd, Wrockwardine Wood. TF2	14 A2	Pavilion Clo. TF	14 D4
New St, Dawley. TF4	17 G6	Pearson Rd. TF2	14 B6
New St, Oakengates. TF2	14 A4	Pemberton Rd. TF5	4 D6
New St, St Georges. TF2	14 B4	Pembridge Clo. TF2	8 D3
New St, Wellington. TF1	11 G3	Pembroke Dri. TF1	12 A2
New Town. TF4	17 G5	Pendil Clo. TF1	11 E4
New Trench Rd. TF2	7 G6	Penistone Clo. TF8	8 C6
New Works La. TF6	16 C3	Perivale Gdns. TF2	9 E4
Newbrookdale. TF1	12 D2	Perry Ct. TF1	11 G1
Newcomen Way. TF7	21 E6	Peters Clo. TF4	21 G1
Newfield Dri. TF2	14 A1	Peveril Bank. TF4	17 G4
Newtonmere Dri. TF1	11 F2	Pickering Rd. TF2	8 A6
Nickless Way. TF4	17 F4	Pickstock Clo. TF3	22 B2
Nightingale Way. TF1	6 B6	Pine View. TF2	8 D4
Norfield Dri. TF3	18 D5	Pinewood Av. TF2	8 A6
North Rd. TF1	11 F2	Pintail Dri. TF1	6 B5
North St. TF2	14 B4	Pitchford Dri. TF2	15 E6
Northwood Ter. TF3	22 B1	Plough Rd, Wrockwardine Wood. TF2	14 B1
Norton Dri. TF3	22 A2	Plough Rd, Wellington. TF1	11 G2
Oak Clo. TF7	22 B6	Plover Gate. TF1	5 E5
Oak Rd. TF3	17 F1	Pool Clo. TF2	7 G6
Oakengates Rd. TF2	8 B6	Pool Farm La. TF1	6 B6
Oakfield Rd. TF5	5 E4	Pool Hill. TF4	21 F1
Oaklands Dri. TF2	8 A5	Pool Hill Rd. TF4	21 E1
Oaks Cres. TF1	11 E5	Pool Meadow. TF1	13 E2
Oakwood Dri. TF2	8 A6	Pool Rd. TF2	13 H1
Old Hall Clo. TF1	12 B4	Pool Side. TF4	17 E5
Old Nursery Clo. TF7	22 A6	Pool View. TF4	16 D6
Old Office Clo. TF4	17 F4	Poplar Clo. TF7	26 B1
Old Office Rd. TF4	17 E4	Poplar Dri. TF1	11 F2
Old Park Rd. TF2	14 A6	Poppy Dri. TF2	8 D5
Old Park Way. TF3	17 G2	Portley Rd. TF4	17 G6
Old Vicarage Rd. TF4	21 G1	Portobello Clo. TF3	17 G1
Old Wharf. TF3	17 H4	Pound La. TF12	25 F6
Oldcroft. TF2	13 H3	Powder La. TF1	11 H3
Oleander Clo. TF3	13 G6	Powell Rd. TF2	15 E5
Oliver Ct. TF1	11 H2	Powis Dri. TF1	11 F2
Onslow Dri. TF1	11 F1	Powis Pl. TF4	17 F3
Orchard Cres. TF1	13 E4	Prestage Clo. TF12	25 F6
Orchard La. TF8	25 E1	Preston Gro. TF2	7 H6
Orchard Way. TF1	12 B3	*Priestland Ter, Furnace La. TF2	8 B5
Orchid Clo. TF2	8 D5	Primmer Rd. TF2	8 C2
Orleton La. TF1	11 F2	Primrose Gro. TF1	12 B4
Orleton Ter. TF1	11 F3	Prince Andrew Dri. TF3	17 H3
Ormsdale Clo. TF2	9 E4	Prince Charles Cres. TF3	17 H3
Osprey Gro. TF1	6 B5	Prince Edward Cres. TF3	17 H3
Osterley Gro. TF2	9 E4	Prince St. TF7	22 B5
Oval Clo. TF2	14 D4	Princes End. TF4	17 F3
Overdale. TF3	13 F6	Princes St. TF1	12 A4
Oxford Rd. TF4	17 G5	Princess Anne Gdns. TF4	17 F6
Oxford St. TF2	14 A4	Princess Av. TF1	12 B4
		Priors Lee Rd. TF11	19 G2
Paddock Clo. TF4	17 G6	Priorslee Av. TF1	14 C6
Paddock Ct. TF4	17 G6	Priorslee Rd. TF2	14 C5
Paddock La. TF11	23 F5	Priorslee Village. TF2	18 D1
Padmans Alley. TF12	24 D5	Priory Ct. TF1	11 H4
Pageant Dri. TF3	21 G2	Priory Rd. TF2	13 H3
Panorama. TF2	14 B3	Proctors Pl. TF2	14 C2
Paradise. TF8	24 C1	Prospect Rd. TF1	11 H3
Parish Clo. TF4	21 F2	Punta Verde. TF7	26 A3
Park Av. TF7	22 A6	Purbeck Dale. TF4	17 F5
Park Clo. TF2	14 D4	Purton Wood View. TF3	18 D5
Park Ct. TF7	21 F5		

30

Street	Ref	Street	Ref	Street	Ref	Street	Ref
Quail Gate. TF1	5 E5	Russell Rd. TF7	22 A6	Sheepwell Ct. TF2	13 G6	Station Rd, Admaston. TF5	4 C6
Quarry La. TF1	13 F4	Russell Sq. TF7	22 A6	Shelley Dri. TF7	26 B2	Station Rd, Coalbrookdale. TF8	20 C6
Quarry Pl.TF4	17 F6	Rutland Grn. TF1	12 C2	Shelsey Ct. TF7	22 A6	Station Rd, Dawley. TF4	17 F5
Quarry Rd. TF12	24 D4	Ryebank Rd. TF2	13 G6	Shepherds Fold. TF4	17 F3	Station Rd, Donnington. TF2	8 C2
Queen Elizabeth Av. TF3	3 C6	Ryton Way. TF3	22 A2	Shepherds La. TF1	13 F4	Station Rd, Ketley. TF1	13 E4
Queen Elizabeth Way. TF3	17 G3			Sheridan Way. TF7	26 C2	Station Rd, Lawley. TF4	17 E3
Queen St, Broseley. TF12	24 D5	Sadlers Fold. TF2	13 H6	Sherlock Hoy Clo. TF12	24 D6	Station Rd, Madeley. TF7	22 A6
Queen St, Madeley. TF7	22 B6	Saggars Clo. TF7	25 F2	Sherwood Clo. TF5	5 F3	Station Rd, Oakengates. TF2	14 A5
Queen St, Wellington. TF1	11 G2	St Agathas Clo. TF1	5 F5	Shetland Clo. TF4	17 E6	Station Rd, Wellington. TF1	11 G3
Queens Rd. TF2	8 C5	St Chads Clo. TF1	11 G1	Shipton Clo. TF3	22 B2	Stebbings. TF7	26 C1
Queens Wood Clo. TF2	3 B1	St Christophers Way. TF4	17 G3	Shrubbery Rd. TF3	13 G5	Steventon Rd. TF1	11 F3
Queensway, Shawbirch. TF1	5 G4	St Davids Clo. TF4	17 G3	Shutfield Rd. TF4	21 G3	Stewardstone Gate. TF2	15 E5
Queensway, Stirchley. TF3	22 A4	St Georges By-Pass. TF2	18 C1	Sidbury Clo. TF3	22 B2	Stile Rise. TF5	5 E4
Queensway, Telford. TF3	3 B1	St Georges Rd, Donnington. TF2	8 C6	Silkin Way, Brattan. TF5	4 D4	Stirchley Av. TF3	3 C6
Queensway, Trench. TF1	13 G1	St Georges Rd, Donnington Wood. TF2	14 C2	Silkin Way, Shawbirch. TF1	5 G5	Stirchley La. TF4	21 H1
Quines Clo. TF2	9 E4	St James Cres. TF3	22 A2	Silkin Way, Stirchley. TF3	22 A1	Stirchley Rd. TF3	22 A2
		St John St. TF1	11 H3	Silverbirch Gro. TF2	9 E4	Stirling Dri. TF7	26 C2
Radnor Ct. TF1	12 C2	St Johns Dri. TF2	14 A1	Silvermere. TF1	14 D6	Stockford Clo. TF2	15 E6
Ragged Robins Clo. TF2	14 C3	St Julians Clo. TF1	5 F5	Silvington. TF3	22 B2	Stockton Clo. TF3	22 B2
Rampart Way.TF3	3 B2	St Leonards Pl. TF4	17 G4	Simon Clo. TF1	11 G3	Stokesay Fore. TF7	26 B3
Randlay Av. TF3	18 C6	St Leonards Rd. TF4	17 G3	Simpsons La. TF12	24 D4	Stokesay Grn. TF7	26 B3
Randlay Fields. TF3	18 C6	St Lukes Rd, Doseley. TF4	21 E2	Sinclair Gdns. TF1	13 E5	Stokesay Link. TF7	26 B2
Ravenhill Dri. TF2	13 G6	St Lukes Rd, Ironbridge. TF8	24 D2	Singleton. TF7	26 C1	Stokesay Rd. TF1	11 F1
Rea Dri. TF1	11 F1	St Margarets Dri. TF1	12 A1	Sixth Av. TF2	3 A1	Stokesay Way. TF7	26 B3
Red Church Clo. TF12	25 F4	St Marks Clo. TF1	5 F5	Slaney St. TF2	14 A4	Stone Cres. TF1	12 C4
Red Lake. TF1	13 F5	St Marys Clo. TF8	25 F3	Small Brook. TF3	17 F2	Stone Row. TF3	17 H4
Red Lane. TF12	25 H6	St Matthews Rd. TF2	8 C6	Smallwood. TF7	26 B2	Stonebridge Clo. TF4	21 H4
Red Lees. TF1	13 E4	St Michaels Clo, Lilleshall. TF10	9 G1	Smarts Way. TF2	14 C4	Stonechat Clo. TF1	12 A1
Redburn Clo. TF2	13 H6	St Michaels Clo, Madeley. TF7	25 H1	Smith Cres. TF2	14 C1	Stonedale. TF7	26 B2
Redfield Clo. TF12	25 E4	St Michaels Dri. TF2	8 A6	Smithy Bank. TF12	24 D5	Stoney Hill. TF7	20 D3
Redhill Way. TF2	14 D2	St Michaels Rd. TF7	25 H1	Snedshill Way. TF2	14 C6	Stowe Clo. TF3	22 B2
Rednal Fields. TF4	21 G2	St Pauls Clo. TF1	5 F5	Snow Hill. TF2	14 C4	Strethill Rd. TF8	24 C1
Redwing Clo. TF1	12 B1	St Quentin Gate. TF3	3 C5	Solway Dri. TF7	26 C2	Stretton Clo. TF7	26 B2
Redwood Clo. TF5	4 D4	Salthouse Rd. TF8	25 G3	Somerset Clo. TF7	25 G1	Strine Clo. TF1	11 F1
Reed Clo. TF2	14 C3	Saltwells Dri. TF2	9 E4	Sommerfeld Rd. TF1	13 F1	Sulby Dri. TF1	12 B1
Regent Dri. TF2	14 C5	Sambrook Clo. TF3	22 B2	South Dri. TF7	25 H1	Summer Cres. TF2	14 B2
Regent Sq. TF7	22 A5	Sandbrook. TF1	12 D3	South View Rd. TF4	21 F3	Summer House Dri. TF1	12 C2
Regent St. TF1	12 A3	Sandcroft. TF2	26 C2	Southall. TF4	21 G2	Summerhill. TF7	26 B1
Reynards Coppice. TF7	26 A2	Sanderstead Ct. TF1	12 D2	Southall Rd. TF4	21 G1	Sunbury Dri. TF2	8 A6
Reynards Meadow. TF7	26 A2	Sanderville Clo. TF3	22 C2	Southfield. TF7	26 B2	Sunderland Dri. TF1	6 C5
Rhodes Av. TF4	17 H4	Sandino Ct. TF3	22 C2	Southgate. TF2	26 B2	Sunningdale. TF1	13 E2
Richards Rd. TF2	8 C2	Sandino Rd. TF3	22 C2	Sovereign Clo. TF4	21 G3	Sunniside. TF8	20 C4
Richmond Av. TF2	8 A6	Sandpiper Clo. TF1	12 B1	Spa Cres. TF5	5 E5	Sunnymead. TF7	26 B1
Richmond Ct. TF1	11 G1	Sandway. TF1	12 D3	Spafield Clo. TF5	5 E4	Sunnyside Rd. TF2	13 G5
Riddings Clo, Broseley. TF12	25 F6	Saxon Ct. TF1	6 C5	Span Meadow. TF5	5 E4	Sutherland Av. TF1	11 H2
Riddings Clo, Ketley. TF1	13 F5	Sceptre Clo. TF1	21 G3	Speeds La. TF12	24 D5	Sutherland Dri. TF2	9 E3
Ringers Way. TF5	4 D6	School Ct. TF1	11 H3	Speedwell Ridge. TF3	18 C6	Sutherland Rd. TF1	11 H2
Ripley Clo. TF1	12 D1	School Gro. TF2	13 H4	Spencer Dri. TF7	26 B2	Sutton Rd. TF5	4 D6
Riverside Av. TF8	26 A4	School La, Ketley. TF1	13 F4	Spinners Ct. TF5	4 D4	Sutton Way. TF7	26 A2
Roberts Rd. TF7	25 E1	School La, Wellington. TF1	11 H4	Spout La. TF6	24 C3	Swallowfield Clo. TF2	15 E6
Robins Dri. TF7	21 E5	School Rd, Coalbrookdale. TF8	20 D5	Spout Way. TF3	3 A6	Swan Gate. TF1	5 E5
Rocfield Ter. TN2	14 A3	School Rd, Donnington. TF2	8 C3	Spring Hill, Dawley. TF4	17 F6	Swan St. TF12	24 D5
Rock Acres. TF10	9 G1	School Rd, Madeley. TF7	25 E1	Spring Hill, Wellington. TF1	11 F2	Swansmede Way. TF3	18 B6
Rock Rd. TF3	13 E5	School St. TF2	14 C4	Spring Meadow. TF7	26 C1	Sweet Briar Clo. TF2	9 E4
Roden Clo. TF1	11 G1	Scott Clo. TF7	26 B2	Spring Ter. TF2	8 B6	Sweet Chestnut Gro. TF3	17 G2
Roman Gro. TF2	14 C4	Second Av. TF2	14 A6	Spring Village. TF4	17 E5	Swift Gate. TF1	5 E5
Rookery Rd. TF2	14 C3	Selbourne. TF7	26 B1	Springfield Clo. TF4	17 G6	Swinburne Clo. TF7	26 B2
Rose Cres. TF1	11 G4	Selkirk Dri. TF7	26 C2	Springfield Rd. TF2	7 G6	Sycamore Clo. TF1	11 E2
Rose Gro. TF1	11 H4	Seven Hills Pl. TF1	13 E3	Springhill Clo. TF7	26 B1	Sycamore Rd. TF12	24 D3
Rose Tree Clo. TF3	13 G6	Severn Bank. TF8	24 D2	Springhill Cres. TF7	26 B1		
Roseway. TF1	11 G3	Severn Dri. TF1	5 F6	Springhill Rd. TF4	17 F5	Tadorna Dri. TF3	22 C2
Roslyn Rd. TF1	11 H2	Severn Ter, Ironbridge. TF8	24 D2	Spruce Dri. TF1	6 C5	Talbot Clo. TF2	14 B1
Rosthwaite. TF1	11 H4	Severn Ter, Jackfield. TF8	25 G3	Squires Clo. TF7	25 G2	Talbot Rd. TF2	14 B1
Rothesay Gro. TF2	13 H6	Severn Walk. TF7	26 B1	Squirrel Meadow. TF5	5 E4	Tamarisk Clo. TF3	13 G6
Rough La. TF2	25 F6	Severn Way. TF1	21 G3	Stadium Way. TF1	13 E2	Tan Bank. TF1	11 G3
Round Oak Dri. TF1	5 G5	Shakespeare Way. TF7	26 B2	Stafford Park Rd. TF3	3 D3	Tarbach Clo. TF12	25 F6
Rowallan Way. TF2	15 E5	Shamrock Way. TF3	18 C6	Stafford Park Way. TF3	18 D5	Teagues Cres. TF2	13 G1
Rowan Av. TF4	21 G1	Shaw La. TF11	19 F6	Stafford Rd. TF2	14 A4	Tee Lake Boulevard. TF1	5 E5
Rowley Clo. TF7	25 G1	Shawbirch Rd. TF5	5 E5	Stafford St. TF2	14 C5	Teece Dri. TF1	15 E6
Rowton Clo. TF1	12 A1			Stallard Ct. TF2	13 G4	Telford Rd, Dawley Bank. TF4	17 H4
Royal Oak Dri. TF1	6 B6			Stanall Dri. TF2	8 D3	Telford Rd, Wellington. TF1	11 F5
Ruith Field. TF5	4 D4			Stanier Dri. TF7	21 E6	Telford Way. TF3	3 D3
Rushbury Rd. TF1	11 E1			Stanley Rd. TF1	11 H3	Teme Av. TF1	5 F6
Rushmoor La. TF5	4 B3			Stanmore Dri. TF7	8 A5		
Ruskin Way. TF3	21 H3			Stanwyck. TF7	26 C1		
				Station Fields. TF2	14 A4		
				Station Hill. TF2	14 B4		

Name	Ref
Tenbury Dri. TF2	8 A6
Teresa Way. TF1	6 B6
Tern Clo. TF4	21 F3
Tern Way. TF1	11 G1
The Avenue, Benthall. TF12	24 B5
The Avenue, Wrockwardine. TF6	10 B2
The Beaches. TF5	4 D6
The Bentlands. TF12	24 C4
The Brambles. TF3	17 G2
The Bungalows. TF2	8 D4
The Cloisters. TF2	13 H3
The Close. TF8	20 C4
The Common. TF2	8 C5
The Court. TF7	26 A3
The Crescent. TF2	8 C4
The Crofts. TF7	21 E5
The Delph. TF3	18 B6
The Fields. TF2	8 D5
The Foxes. TF7	26 A2
The Grove Est. TF2	14 C5
The Hay. TF3	17 F2
The Incline. TF1	13 F5
The Knowle. TF8	25 F3
The Lawns. TF1	11 G2
The Ley. TF4	21 G1
The Lloyds. TF8	25 F2
The Meadows, Ketley Bank. TF2	13 H5
The Meadows, Lawley. TF4	16 D3
The Mines. TF12	24 D3
The Nabb. TF2	14 B3
The Paddock. TF2	9 E4
The Parade, Donnington. TF2	8 C5
The Parade, Wellington. TF1	11 G3
The Pippins. TF3	18 C6
The Rock. TF3	17 F1
The Rookery. TF7	22 A6
The Savannahs. TF1	5 G5
The Square. TF8	24 D2
The Stables. TF2	9 E4
The Stockings. TF4	21 E3
The Wharfage. TF8	24 C1
The Woodlands. TF2	14 B2
Third Av. TF2	3 B1
Thirlmere Gro. TF2	14 D6
Thistle Clo. TF3	18 C5
Thornton Park Av. TF2	9 E4
Toll Rd. TF1	12 B5
Tontine Hill. TF8	24 D2
Trafalgar Clo. TF1	8 D3
Trench Clo. TF2	7 G6
Trench Lock. TF1	13 F1
Trench Lock 1. TF1	13 F1
Trench Lock 2. TF1	13 F1
Trench Lock 3. TF1	13 G1
Trench Lock 5. TF1	13 G2
Trench Rd. TF2	7 G6
Trenleigh Gdns. TF2	13 H1
Trinity Rd. TF4	21 F2
Trinity View. TF2	13 H5
Troon Way. TF7	26 B3
Tudor Meadow. TF2	7 G6
Turnpike Ct. TF2	14 C4
Turnstone Dri. TF1	12 C2
Turreff Av. TF2	8 C4
Tweedale Court. TF7	22 B5
Tweedale Cres. TF7	22 B5
Tweedale North. TF7	22 B5
Tweedale South. TF7	22 B5
Tynsley Ct. TF7	22 A6
Tynsley Ter. TF7	22 A6
Ullswater Clo. TF2	14 C6
Undertrees Clo. TF1	5 G5
Underwood. TF12	25 E4
Union Ct. TF1	13 E2
Union Rd, Wellington. TF1	11 G4
Union Rd, Wrockwardine Wood. TF2	14 A2
Uplands Av. TF2	13 H3
Upper Dingle. TF2	25 F2
Upper Rd. TF7	22 A6
Upper Wood. TF3	17 F2
Urban Gdns. TF1	12 B3
Urban Rd. TF2	14 A2
Urban Villas. TF2	14 C4
Urban Way. TF1	12 B3
Valley Rd, Arleston. TF1	12 B5
Valley Rd, Overdale. TF3	17 F1
Verbena Way. TF7	26 A2
Vicar St. TF2	13 H4
Victoria Av, Ketley. TF1	12 D3
Victoria Av, Wellington. TF1	11 H3
Victoria Ct. TF1	13 E2
Victoria Rd, Madeley. TF7	21 H6
Victoria Rd, Wellington. TF1	11 G3
Victoria St. TF1	11 H3
Viewlands Dri. TF2	8 A5
Villa Ct. TF7	22 A6
Village Ct. TF2	18 D1
Vineyard Dri. TF1	11 G2
Violet Clo. TF2	9 E4
Viscount Av. TF4	21 H3
Wade Rd. TF2	14 B1
Wadham Clo. TF1	12 A1
Waggoners Fold. TF3	17 H4
Wagtail Dri. TF4	21 H3
Walder Clo. TF4	17 F5
Walker Cres. TF2	14 B3
Walker St. TF1	11 G3
Walney Ct. TF7	21 F6
Walsh Clo. TF2	15 E5
Walton Av. TF6	13 H3
Waltondale. TF7	21 G6
Wantage. TF7	21 G5
Warrensway. TF7	21 E6
Waterloo Clo. TF2	13 E3
Waterloo Rd, Ketley. TF1	13 E2
Waterloo Rd, Wellington. TF1	11 H3
Waterloo St. TF8	25 E2
Watling St. TF1	12 B4
Waverley. TF7	21 G5
Wavertree Clo. TF2	14 B4
Waxhill Clo. TF2	8 D6
Wayside. TF7	21 G6
Wealdstone. TF7	21 F5
Weavers Rise. TF2	13 H5
Webb Cres. TF4	21 F1
Wedgwood Cres. TF1	12 D3
Weir Gdns. TF1	13 E1
Wellington Rd, Admaston. TF5	4 D6
Wellington Rd, Coalbrookdale. TF8	20 C5
Wellington Rd, Donnington. TF2	8 B4
Wellington Rd, Lawley. TF4	16 D3
Wellsfield. TF7	21 G5
Wellswood Av. TF2	3 B1
Wenlock Ct. TF7	21 F6
Wesley Dri. TF2	13 H5
Wesley Rd. TF8	25 E2
West Av. TF2	8 B5
West Centre Way. TF4	17 G2
West Rd, Ketley Bank. TF2	13 G5
West Rd, Wellington. TF1	11 F3
West St. TF2	14 C4
West View Ter. TF7	21 G6
Westbourne. TF7	21 F6
Westerdale Clo. TF4	21 F1
Westerkirk Dri. TF7	25 G1
Western Rise. TF1	12 D3
Westmorland Mews. TF1	12 C2
Weston Dri. TF1	11 F2
Weybridge. TF7	21 E6
Weyman Rd. TF1	11 F1
Wharf Clo. TF2	14 B4
Wheatley Cres. TF1	6 D6
Wheeldale Clo. TF4	21 E1
Whimbrel Clo. TF1	12 C1
Whinchat Clo. TF1	12 B1
Whitchurch Dri, Shawbirch. TF1	5 G5
Whitchurch Dri, Wellington. TF1	12 A1
Whitchurch Rd. TF1	11 G1
White Horse Clo. TF4	17 F4
Whitebeam Clo. TF3	17 G1
Whitehall Gdns. TF12	25 E6
Whitemere Rd. TF1	11 F2
Whitington Clo. TF2	14 A3
Whitmore Clo. TF12	25 F6
Whitworth Dri. TF3	18 B6
Wicket Clo. TF2	14 D4
Widewaters Clo. TF4	21 G3
Wigmores. TF7	21 G5
Wild Thyme Dri. TF2	8 D4
Wildwood. TF7	21 F5
Wilkinson Av. TF12	25 E6
Willetts Way. TF4	17 F4
Williams Rd. TF2	8 C2
Willow Bank. TF4	21 H3
Willow Rd. TF2	14 B4
Willowfield. TF7	21 G5
Wilmere Ct. TF7	21 F6
Windermere Dri. TF2	14 C6
Windsor Cres. TF12	24 D4
Windsor Pl. TF4	17 F6
Windsor Rd, Arleston. TF1	12 C4
Windsor Rd, Dawley. TF4	17 F6
Winifreds Dri. TF2	8 B5
Winston Dri. TF2	8 C4
Withybrook. TF7	21 E5
Withywood Dri. TF3	3 A5
Wolverley Ct. TF7	21 F5
Wombridge Rd, Trench. TF2	7 H6
Wombridge Rd, Wombridge. TF2	13 G3
Wombridge Way. TF2	13 G4
Wood Clo. TF2	8 C6
Woodbine Clo. TF2	8 D4
Woodcroft. TF7	21 G5
Woodford Grn. TF5	5 E4
Woodhall Clo. TF5	4 D4
Woodhouse. TF2	15 E6
Woodhouse Central. TF3	3 B4
Woodhouse Clo. TF2	15 E5
Woodhouse Cres. TF2	8 A6
Woodhouse La, Horsehay. TF4	16 D6
Woodhouse La, Priorslee. TF2	15 E5
Woodhouse La, Redhill. TF2	15 G2
Woodhouse Rd. TF12	24 D5
Woodland Villas. TF2	14 B2
Woodlands Av. TF1	11 F3
Woodlands Clo. TF12	24 D3
Woodlands Grn. TF12	24 D4
Woodlands La. TF4	20 D2
Woodlands Rd. TF8	25 E2
Woodrows. TF7	21 G5
Woodrush Heath. TF3	17 G2
Woodside. TF8	20 D5
Woodside Av. TF7	21 F5
Woodside Clo. TF1	13 E5
Woodside Rd. TF1	13 E4
Woodwell. TF1	13 G5
Woollam Rd. TF1	12 C4
Worcester Rd. TF4	17 G5
Wordsworth Way. TF2	14 D6
Worfe Clo. TF3	18 D5
Wrekin Clo. TF2	7 G6
Wrekin Dri. TF2	8 B5
Wrekin Rd. TF1	11 G3
Wrekin View, Madeley. TF7	25 F1
Wrekin View, Wrockwardine. TF6	10 B2
Wrens Nest La. TF1	13 E5
Wrockwardine Rd. TF1	11 E2
Wrockwardine Wood Way. TF2	14 A2
Wroxeter Way. TF3	22 C2
Wych Elm Dri. TF5	5 F4
Wyke La. TF12	24 A5
Wyke Rise. TF1	12 A1
Wyvern. TF7	21 E6
Yates Way. TF2	3 A1
Yew Tree Clo. TF7	25 G2
Yew Tree Dri. TF10	9 G2